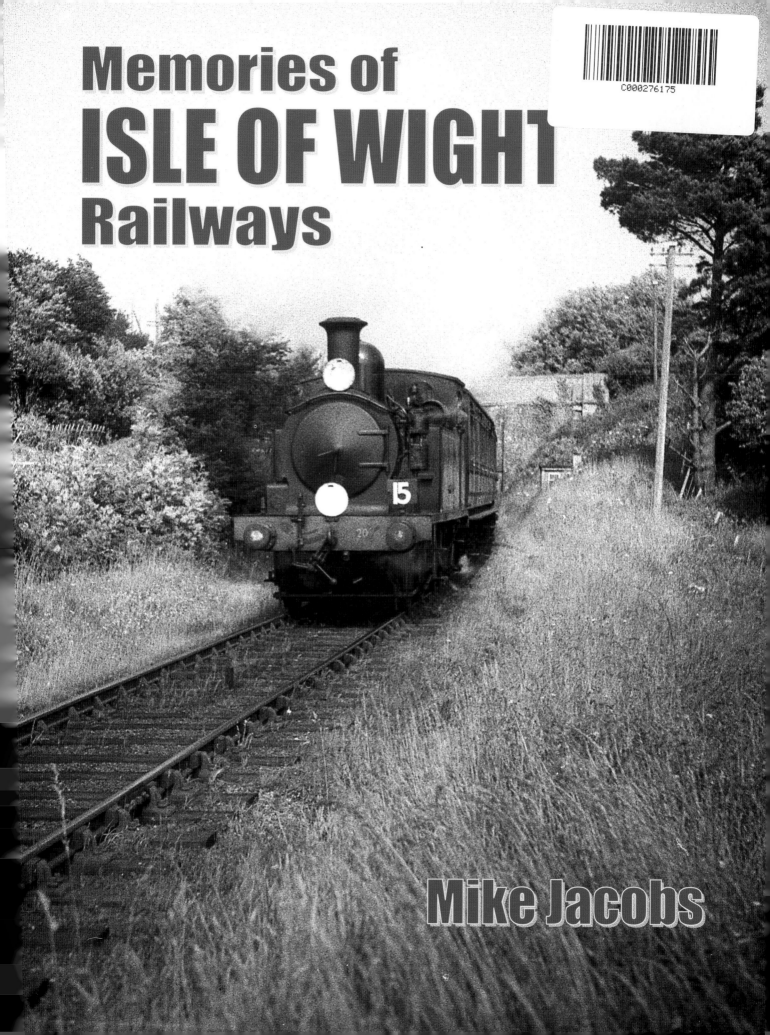

Memories of
ISLE OF WIGHT
Railways

Mike Jacobs

© Noodle Books and Mike Jacobs 2010   ISBN 978-1-906419-36-3

First published in 2010 by Kevin Robertson under the **NOODLE BOOKS** imprint
PO Box 279 Corhampton, SOUTHAMPTON SO32 3ZX

www.noodlebooks.co.uk

Printed in England by The Information Press.

INTRODUCTION

I put together the original draft of the this work in the mid-1990's, and much of the text appeared in serial form some years ago in "Island Rail News", the quarterly journal of the Isle of Wight Steam Railway, as did a few of the photographs. After this, these written memories languished until they were read by an old friend of mine, and fellow Isle of Wight Railways enthusiast, Frank Spence. Frank was generous enough to make kind comments, and later put me in touch with the publisher, Kevin Robertson. The result is this book. I owe a great debt of gratitude to both gentlemen: to Frank for his encouragement, to Kevin for his support, and to both of them for their unflagging enthusiasm.

For its publication now as a complete work I have edited and added to the original text, and we have incorporated many hitherto unpublished photographs, including some splendid images from the camera of the late Denis Callender, reproduced with permission of Jonny Callender. We have also included a selection of colour images from various sources at the end of the volume. I very much hope that the result will enable the reader to share some of my fascination with the Island's railway system, and perhaps understand a little of the love that I had, and still have, for the lines as they were in my younger days.

Mike Jacobs
Lustleigh
Devon

May 2010

All unaccredited views were taken by the Author.

Front cover, top - *Ventnor West, 7 May 1950. Set 503, former LBSCR stock, is in the platform.*   *Denis Callender*

Front cover, bottom - *Sandown, No. 27 'Merstone' is on a Ventnor train.*   *John Bailey*

Rear cover - *A rare colour view of one of the Island 'E1' 0-6-0Ts', this example No. W4 'Wroxall', in company with an unidentified 'O2', at Ryde St Johns depot in the late 1950s.*   *W Kellaway*

Frontispiece - *No. 20 'Shanklin' passing the site of Apse Siding, between Shanklin and Wroxall, 28 June 1958.*

Opposite page - *Smallbrook Junction, No. 18 'Osborne' on a Ventnor train, 20 May 1961.*

Top - Southern Railway paddle-steamer 'Merstone'. Built in 1928, along with her sister vessel 'Portsdown', they replaced the 'Duchess of Albany' and 'Princess Margaret' both of which were sold for breaking up. The new boats had a large deckhouse and skylight that provided both light and ventilation to the engine room. During WW2 'Merstone' was used as a troop transport for naval personnel being taken to their ships in preparation for 'D-day'. 'Merstone' survived the conflict although 'Portsdown' was not so lucky, being sunk by a mine in 1941. After the war, 'Merstone' continued the service from Portsmouth to the Isle of Wight until 1952, when she was withdrawn following the introduction of the new motor vessels 'Shanklin' and 'Brading.' 'Merstone' was then laid up and finally sold for scrap in September 1952. In service, she had an operational speed of 13.5 knots.

RCHS - Spence collection

Bottom - David Hammersley collection

Memories of ISLE OF WIGHT Railways

Like many events in a past viewed from late-ish middle-age, it's hard to know where this Isle of Wight business all began.

I think that it was all father's fault, really. His was a fairly typical London family of the late Victorian and Edwardian era, which, like many of similar ilk, viewed the annual holiday on the South Coast as one of the more important events of the year. Their addiction to resorts was not entirely slavish, and Margate, Deal, Folkestone, Hastings and Southsea featured from time to time in the itinerary. Listening to father, though, it always seemed to me as a child that most of his favourite times were spent on the Isle of Wight, and I grew up in my early years, even when I had hardly visited the place, knowing from my father's tales that it was somewhere pleasant where good things happened.

I had, for as long as I can remember (and further back still, so I'm told), nurtured a liking for railways, which, as I got older, turned into something of an obsession. It wasn't only the usual juvenile acquisitiveness of collecting locomotive numbers, although that featured for a long time as part of the rigmarole, but an involvement which eventually embraced almost every area of the subject. As I grew, railways provided me with a vestigial knowledge of mechanical, electrical and civil engineering, sociology, business management and economics, all overlaid by an intense love of the countryside and the movement of trains through it.

Small wonder, then, that the Isle of Wight grabbed me from the moment I first set foot there, and my existing loves were enhanced by the special magic that only those who have become involved with the place and its railways will understand.

I know I first visited the Island - just - it was only the beach at Ryde - in 1945. At that time my father was working at Portsmouth Dockyard and we lived in Southsea, and several times that year my mother gathered up my brother, sister and myself, to meet the old man at the Dockyard gates when he finished work. From there it was an easy step past the remains of the South Railway Jetty viaduct to Portsmouth Harbour Station, where we embarked on one of the ferries for an evening trip to Ryde.

The name "Merstone" sticks in my mind, and I remember riding the paddle steamer, totally fascinated, as I was for years afterwards on other vessels, with the business of paddlewheels and the beautiful and mighty machinery (viewed from a window into the engine room) which drove them. "Merstone" was still in war time grey, and I have some recollections of coal dust and the smell of steam and a tall funnel venting black smoke.

The Isle of Wight, for that is how Ryde was understood by me in those days (I seemed not to observe the hills beyond the town for a year or two), was dominated by the Pier. Which interested child could have resisted the procession of trains to and from the Pier Head, or the trundling trams on the adjacent tracks? Riding them seemed unimportant. It was their presence which cast the spell, even as far as my not wanting to play on the beach unless it was close to, or - even better - underneath the Pier.

During our walks along the length of the Pier heading either for beach or return ferry home, the trains seemed innumerable. They couldn't have been, of course. This was still war time. But to a youthful railway lover whose usual diet was nine-tenths Southern Electric - and quite nice, too, but not very exciting - all this steam activity seemed larger than life. I can remember the rumble under my feet as they passed, and watching the trains heading down the line towards the direction I later recognised of Ventnor or Newport. For some reason, the rear profile of the carriages stays with me, dark and LSWR-shaped, although this sharpness may have been heightened by subsequent acquaintance. The Pier trams on their separate tracks added another dimension of interest of a kind hitherto undiscovered, although I was unsure about their being described as "trams" because my one visit to Southampton had demonstrated these to me as things that ran through the streets of towns.

1946 saw further visits to Ryde, and the initial fascination scarcely wore off, although trips in other directions had

given the Pier a rival in the form of the wooden bridge which separated Hayling Island from the mainland.

In 1947 I realised that there was territory beyond Ryde, when the family made an excursion as far as my father's old stamping ground of Shanklin. And what territory it was, with rolling countryside and woods and glimpses of the sea and stations at which we passed other trains. Little of this journey remains in memory, probably because it was overshadowed by the fact that I distinguished myself by being seasick on the ferry, and, more pleasantly, by the sunshine, the cliffs and the momentous first ice cream (remember, the war was not long over)! The little trains had, however, increased their hold.

The next return to the Island was in 1949, and this was a year of many visits. Still living in the Portsmouth area, my parents took massive advantage of our proximity to Wight and the numerous special fares available from what was, by now, British Railways, Southern Region. This latter state of affairs was not easy for me to grasp, requiring a quantum leap in thinking of which I was not at that time capable. The business of ownership was incomprehensible and unimportant, and trains were things that, well, just existed. That was the important thing. And they were headed by interesting locomotives on sunny days. That they carried things was taken for granted, but the understanding of the underlying economics and sociology were some years off. It went without saying that the best locomotives were green (or sometimes black), and that they had "Southern" written upon their tank sides or tenders - that kind of loyalty I was grasping - although I remember seeing some tempting things elsewhere on trips to London to see relatives.

It was 1949 that finally sealed the knot of what has become a lifetime's love affair with the Island and its railways. That year we mainly used the then new diesel ferries "Brading" and "Southsea" to get to the Island. These were more comfortable than their paddle-driven predecessors, but not nearly so interesting. I was pleased as the years unrolled that a few of the paddle-steamers survived, along with their floating bunkering facility in Portsmouth harbour. Once on the Island, we not only visited Ryde again, but also went to Sandown, Shanklin, Ventnor, Bembridge, and on one incredible journey, to Newport as well. The numbers and names of locomotives were collected, and every member of the fleet then extant, except for one of the two remaining A1X's, was seen. This bag included the errant E4 0-6-2T 2510, which must have been observed shortly before its return to the mainland.

I got to know the Ventnor line well, and can recall glimpses of a number of things. There was the Bembridge branch train, the engine of which always seemed to be hiding behind shrubs at the south end of the down platform at Brading, and a coach with a corridor connection parked on the nearby Chalk Siding. There was a flat wagon of some description which remained on what I came to know later as the IWCR sidings at Sandown (the official name was Brickfield Sidings) for the duration of several visits, freshly painted in Southern green, with "SR" in gold. Many years later I learned that this was the solitary and unique boat wagon.

At Shanklin there was the murky subway and the "Best Kept Station" seat, upon which we sat at the north end of the platform in the late afternoon sun whilst awaiting the train to Ryde. Once or twice we forsook the train at Shanklin and headed out on foot over the downs to Ventnor, watching the trains as they scurried round the foot of St Martin's Down, and marvelling, when we got there, at Ventnor Station, nestling in the bottom of its well in St Boniface Down, and, on the way home, at the length of the tunnel connecting it with the rest of the world.

On one trip to Ventnor we walked out towards the west, seeing from a distance the push-pull train from Ventnor West to Merstone making its quiet way along the Undercliff, headed I think by No 35, which at that time must have been a very new arrival indeed in the Island. Later, we found St Lawrence station, smothered in the quietude of the sparsely served branch line, and I smelt for the first time I can remember that unique and beautiful branch line aroma of wild flowers and grass mingled with sleeper creosote, as we gazed over the platform fence watching young rabbits playing in the sunshine on the side of the cutting beyond.

The ride to Bembridge was so full of interest that I could scarcely contain my desire to have all these railways to myself, to discover and cherish. The branch locomotive was real after all, and didn't spend all its time hiding behind the shrubbery at the end of the bay platform at Brading. There were two coaches, and the two and three quarter mile run might have been short on distance, but it was long on pure delight. St Helen's Quay, absolutely full of rolling stock, staggered, but the discovery of the turntable at Bembridge beat everything else that day, and I spent a long time watching its use as a means of releasing the locomotive to run round the train. Watching the engine crew using the white painted locking levers to push the turntable into motion, I was a little saddened that the locomotive was not turned completely, and that this perfectly good mechanism was only used like a pair of points. But that notwithstanding, the Island had a turntable. A look across the harbour to the St. Helen's side revealed what seemed like an enormous number of old coaches, grounded to make huts for bathing. They were still green, but having no wheels, did not spark too much interest. If only I had known that they were probably the largest surviving collection of ex-Metropolitan non-bogie eight wheelers, I might have paid them more regard, but in those days of callowness, I doubt it!

Then another time there was the journey to Newport, through more fresh countryside. Except for a long line of empty open wagons on the siding at Ashey, I recall little of the journey, but the expanse and business of Newport is still

Opposite page - Ryde Pier Head, with Pier Tramway Motor Car No. 1 and Trailer No. 8. 19 May 1961.

Merstone, 7 August 1950. In the right hand platform (officially No. 1 Road), is No. 25 'Godshill' with a through working from Cowes to Ventnor via Sandown. Trains to and from Sandown and Newport were able to use either platform because both were signalled for bi-directional working. However, trains to and from Ventnor West could only use No. 2 Road, the junction for the Ventnor West line being to the left behind the photographer. Denis Callender

a photographic image. There seemed so much going on. A continual procession of trains to almost everywhere else on the Island (at that time I harboured a mistaken impression that the Ventnor West branch connected directly with the Island's capital!), the curious antics of the trains to Freshwater - nothing in my experience ever reversed out of a station to get where it wanted to go to! - and the movements of locomotives around the yards and shed. Clearly, with its acres of sidings, Newport was a station to be reckoned with, and it figured large in my personal railway lore for years afterwards.

That year it seemed as if all the locomotives were still in Southern green, applied with the artistic Island finish of edging and lining, and kept much cleaner than those on the mainland. Of course, they were not all like that, but even if some I saw were lettered "British Railways", the green still ruled, and I suppose that might have been the start of my belief that Island people, railway workers and public alike, regarded their trains as something special and unique.

The period of the next two or three years was a fallow patch in my pursuit of the Island's lines. We moved to London, and other railway interests intervened. In spite of this, there were many times, particularly on sunny days, when I

dreamed of open downland with carpets of vetch and lady's slipper and knolls of gorse and hawthorn, and views of trains below. London Transport, the GC & Metropolitan Joint and the LNW main line had their charms, but they couldn't really compete with the south country that I had become used to, and the special charms of that isolated diamond of land across the Solent.....

In 1953 a family holiday was decided upon, and there was unanimous delight that the Isle of Wight was chosen. Shanklin was to be headquarters, and a boarding house was duly booked for a week at the end of August.

Surprise. When we reached Ryde Pier Head, all the engines were in BR black, and the coaches in standard crimson. But once I got over this, it was soon apparent that nothing else had changed very much. Except that there were clouds looming. My father had drawn my attention to a short item in the paper a year previously reporting the closure of the railway to Ventnor West, but it had meant little. I had no real knowledge of the line, except for St. Lawrence and the rabbits. Now, however, there was devastation nearer at hand, and notices were posted announcing the impending doom of the Bembridge and the Freshwater branches. To be sure, I didn't know much about the Freshwater route, except

Above - No. 20 'Shanklin' arriving at Brading with a Sandown train, with No. 31 'Chale' awaiting departure for Ryde. 25 July 1959.

Left - Brading Signal Box circa 1950, which at its peak contained a 30 lever frame with just one spare.

Denis Callender

This page, top - St. Helen's looking west towards Brading. The connection leading to the North and South Quay sidings is on the right.

Right - No. 20 'Shanklin' entering St. Helen's from Bembridge.

Opposite, top - Just east of St. Helen's, the train is about to cross the bridge over the River Yar.

Opposite, bottom - St. Helen's, from Station Road.
All by Denis Callender in the early 1950s.

11

St. Helen's Quay

Scenes at St. Helen's Quay

Opposite page, top - The engine shed probably dated from the opening of the Bembridge branch in 1884 and was always a sub-shed of Ryde who supplied a locomotive to be out-stationed here. This practice ceased and the shed was closed in 1921.
Opposite page, bottom - The former goods offices.   *Both by Denis Callender in the early 1950s.*
This page, top - View of the entrance to St. Helen's Quay showing tracks diverging to the North and South Quay.
This page, bottom - Rolling stock in the process of being scrapped on the South Quay, with the wagon turntable in the foreground. *Both 23 April 1957.*

Top - *Ex-Metropolitan eight-wheeled non-bogie coach bodies used as beach huts on the Duver at St Helen's 15 April 1960. The body nearest the camera is composite, Southern No. 6340, withdrawn in 1928.*

This page, centre and bottom - *The office and goods shed at St. Helen's Quay.*   *Denis Callender*

Opposite page - *Admiring glances for No. 14 Fishbourne on the engine release turntable at Bembridge. May 1952.*   *Denis Callender*

that it had provided my parents with a holiday in 1939 (they stayed in a grounded, converted and connected pair of ex-Freshwater, Yarmouth and Newport Railway coaches near Yarmouth), but it did feature in the plans for this holiday. But how could anyone contemplate extinguishing the line to Bembridge, with its access to all those carriages and wagons on St. Helens Quay?

We couldn't get to Bembridge - arrangements didn't allow it, in spite of my best efforts to get them changed - except by a brief stop in a 'bus journey, and I remembering looking over the fence at the station and turntable and feeling sad and confused and disbelieving. Alas, I still had not grasped some of the economic facts of life.

Still, we did manage two trips on the still crowded and popular "Tourist" through train. Each time we boarded it at Shanklin, and rode to Newport non-stop, with only a pause at Sandown, behind an E1 0-6-0T. On one of journeys I know that the locomotive was No 1. The journey across the middle of the Island seemed largely a procession of little stations, each with a level crossing and a siding. At Merstone, altogether bigger, as befitted a junction station (my geography of the Island lines was now more accurate) watch was kept for the Ventnor West line, which sure enough came curving in from the south, rusty, but not with the brown rust of long neglect, more the orange variety which seemed to me to indicate that things still ventured down the rails from time to time. One of the sidings at Merstone contained empty steel ballast wagons which by the time we took our second trip had migrated to the siding at Blackwater where they were being loaded with ballast from a conveyor.

Soon there was the activity of Newport. Whilst I wished for more than one pair of eyes so that I could watch everything, we stopped at the station, and then gently pulled forward to clear the entrance to the Freshwater line, stopping to exchange our E1 for an O2. Then we were off again, bustling through virgin territory towards West Wight, with trees

The solitary IOW horsebox, of LBSCR vintage, at Yarmouth. Sent to the Island in 1925 it was given the number 3370 in 1929 but saw little use. Even so it was repainted in malachite green in 1945 and subsequently fully overhauled in 1950. A further works visit in 1952 saw BR crimson applied and the number given an 'S' prefix. With the closure of the Freshwater line in 1953, the vehicle was removed to St. Helen's Quay, where it was eventually broken up.   *Denis Callender*

brushing the windows, halting briefly at Ningwood to pass another train. Here I thought I'd discovered oil tank wagons, but later knowledge told me that the two black hulks parked at the end of the siding were the IWCR water tanks, converted for weed-killing by the Southern.

Half the passengers decamped at Yarmouth, ourselves amongst them. Returning to the station at the end of the day, I was struck by the curious staggered nature of the platforms. Of course, the down one had not been used for many years and had no track, but it was obvious that when the rails had been in position the western points of the loop must have been halfway along the main platform. This did not seem right or logical at all, not from my understanding of passing loops, anyway. The single siding was surrounded by a grassy goods yard, and besides the odd open wagon or two, was host to a van-like vehicle finished in crimson. I discovered later that it was the solitary Isle of Wight (ex-LBSCR) horse-box near the end of its days.

Eventually, the return "Tourist" came rattling over the causeway by the River Yar, and once more installed, we wended our way back to Shanklin in late afternoon sunlight.

The second trip a couple of days later allowed me to confirm all my previous observations, and although we again alighted at Yarmouth, this time we walked to Freshwater and picked up the return working there. Few recollections remain of Freshwater station, except that the single platform seemed exceedingly long, and for some reason the standard Southern pre-cast concrete fence along its length made an impression on me.

Little more remains of the magical week, except a feeling of something like loss which gradually crept over me as we sped back to London ensconced in our 4-COR electric unit, but I had a distinct sensation that for no particular reason I could fathom, that some kind of change in family life was afoot. In the slightly longer term, I was right. We took up residence at Ventnor in the early autumn of 1954.

Thus ended the formative period of my association with the Isle of Wight and its railways. The next five years, as well as being a generally enjoyable trip through my adolescence, enabled me to become one of that rare and lucky group of people who were almost daily users of the Island's railways. My obsession did not diminish one jot. In fact, it grew.

Views from, and of 'The Tourist', early September 1953.

Above - The crew of No. 1, 'Medina' pose after the arrival at Newport of 'the Tourist' from Ventnor.
Right - Approaching Ningwood where it will cross a train for Freshwater.
Centre, left and right - Arriving at and departing from Yarmouth.
Bottom - Between Yarmouth and Freshwater, viewed across the marshes of the estuary of the western Yar.

A Freshwater train at Newport, 1953, with No. 31 'Chale'.
RCHS Spence collection

The next visits to the Island were for house-hunting, in the late summer of 1954. The obvious choice of Shanklin, home, in a sense because of father's youthful holidays, to our whole Island legend, was for some reason discarded, and eventually a bungalow at Ventnor, high up on the Whitwell Road, was purchased.

The house-hunting visits were day trips. A more business-like view of the railways was acquired. After all, they were to become part of everyday life. Bustling black engines, crimson coaches in the sharp sunlight of mornings in the decline of the summer, and lengthening early shadows on return trips. For some reason, a particular memory of yellow ballast tipped down an embankment between Smallbrook and Brading, presumably to halt subsidence or to reinforce the earthworks.

And then the irrevocable step. The family, or most of them, arriving at Ventnor in early October, cluttered with hand luggage and a recalcitrant and difficult ginger tomcat who had cried noisily for freedom ever since we had left North London. Sudden realisation that this was it - from now on, we were Isle of Wight residents, and the trains were mine.

For some reason there was a delay in my acquiring a place at school. Sandown Grammar was to be my *alma mater* until I finished education, but some administrative hiccup prevented my immediate start, and I was given an unexpected holiday of a fortnight. Once able to escape from the domestic turmoil of taking up residence, I set about exploring, and before long was heading in the direction of the Ventnor West line, just to view the rusting remains (and, I suspect, in a rapidly encroaching winter of bare trees and early darkness, to remind myself of sunshine and rabbits).

I walked from Ventnor along the Undercliff to St Lawrence, found the station and looked over the fence. I was not prepared for what I saw. No railway, just freshly turned ballast where the sleepers had been, a weed-grown platform and a derelict building. Perhaps I ought to have known, but I still had a gap in my mind which said that railways were fixtures, always there. They might be disused, but they remained in situ. To find a railway destroyed was an impossibility which forced me to re-map my world with dismay. Later, we frequently used a bridle path which led from the upper road on which we lived down to the Undercliff through dense undergrowth and tall trees dangling ivy like

tropical lianas, and had to pass between the open abutments of a bridge under the railway. Again it seemed to me that there was something not quite right. Railways were big and heavy, and removing their furniture was a step too radical to contemplate, irrevocable in its immensity. Even then, I suppose, I harboured some vision of a return to rail which would reinvigorate slumbering lines. Alas, there were to be many span-less bridge abutments to be viewed before the trickle of reawakening started in the 1970's.

The saving grace of the miserable expedition to St Lawrence was the discovery on the bridge where the road called the Shute crossed the railway adjacent to the station of a cast iron notice, laying down restrictions on road traffic in the name of the Isle of Wight Central Railway. (I later discovered that it was the twin of a similar notice on the bridge at Wootton station.) This was exciting, and gave a glimpse of Island railway prehistory that I had not yet given much thought to.

Later during my enforced holiday I found my way to Ventnor West station, similarly derelict and overgrown, and on a second visit to St Lawrence, capitalising on the fact that the trackbed seemed to be used as a footpath, walked up to the mouth of the tunnel under the down. I ventured inside, but with the curve rapidly eliminating the daylight, I abandoned exploration, and turned around. It was all too quiet.

Finally, my day for starting school was agreed, and I was escorted by mother on the train to Sandown. I remember each compartment seemed full to overflowing with children of all sizes, all in the dark and light blue uniform of Sandown Grammar School. They seemed to take the journey to school very much for granted, as we all eventually did. The frightening introduction to my new educational home - co-ed, Latin, two sites separated by half a mile - over, I began to see how the life of Sandown Grammar was to some extent governed by the railway.

There seemed to be three sorts of child, known respectively as Ryde train, Newport train and Ventnor train, and the whole business of getting pupils to and from school was organised with a military exactness. The first to arrive in the morning were those from the Newport line, followed by those from Ryde, with the Ventnor line contingent bringing up the rear. On Mondays, school started early, with a registration and dinner-money collection period before assembly,

Opposite - Local traffic was still good, even in the latter days of steam. Here there is brisk business at Wroxall, with passengers having alighted from a train for Ventnor, 9 May 1959.

The Ventnor West branch.

Top - St Lawrence looking towards Ventnor West. May 1951.

Left - The south portal of the 619 yard St Lawrence Tunnel. May 1952.

Opposite top - The station seen from the approach road. Pedestrian and vehicle access was from Castle Road which in turn led off Park Avenue. The building on the extreme left was Pickford's store. 7 August 1950.

Opposite right - Looking towards Merstone. The signal box contained 13 levers. 7 August 1950.

All by Denis Callender

The Ventnor West Branch

High summer at Ventnor West, 1950. The station was originally called 'Ventnor Town', but the name was changed by the Southern in 1923. From this angle it is hard to believe that the location was a mere branch terminus, because the picture gives the impression of something more grandiose. On the extreme left is a glimpse of the goods shed which was served by a second siding, which also dealt with coal. The short siding on the right gave access to a loading bank and cattle dock, and was also sued for locomotive servicing.

Denis Callender

Above - The approach to Ventnor West. The signals are from the top, 'Up Signal to Platform No. 1', 'Up Signal to Platform No. 2' and 'Up Signal to Sidings and Yard'. As the yard was to the left of the running line (where the open wagons can be seen) this arrangement contradicts the normally held practice of 'Top to Bottom: Left to Right' applicable to stop arms below each other on the same post. Since Southern Railway days economy had been effected, with the signalling arranged so that the home and starting signals could be left in the 'off' position, as now, with the relevant points locked and pull-push working by long-section 'staff and ticket'.

Opposite top - Former LBSCR saloon brake composite, No. 6986 - later converted by British Railways to breakdown van DS70008, stabled on the goods shed siding. Spare coaching stock was often kept in this location

Opposite bottom - The north end of St Lawrence tunnel and distant signal for Dean Crossing, apparently viewed from the driver's vestibule of a push-pull train..

All by Denis Callender in the early 1950s.

Right - No. 14 'Fishbourne' arriving at Shanklin with a Ventnor train - Mike Jacobs' first ever photograph as an Island resident. 12 May 1956.

Opposite page - A platelayer looks on thoughtfully as No. 28 'Ashey' prepares to leave Brading. 25 July 1959.

and this meant the rigours of a start from Ventnor a minute or two before 8.00am instead of the usual 8.40. In the afternoon Ryde was first to leave the station, followed quickly by Newport. The Ventnor kids had to hang on until 4.26pm, and were not allowed to leave the precincts of the school until a bell had been rung at around 4.15. The daily late departure from Sandown to Ventnor was to some extent offset by the fact that the Friday after-school detention for bad conduct had to give way to the next convenient train, which was at 4.46pm, so in effect one had only to do twenty minutes for misdemeanours!

Pupils were not allowed freedom of movement on the train until they were in the fifth form. Lists were published every year for each train, dividing the children into various groups, each of which was expected to use one compartment under the watchful eye of a fifth or sixth-former glorying in the title of "Train Prefect". These last were people of some authority (although not as much as fully-fledged prefects) and had the power to dish out lines as punishment for unruliness on the train! Girls were always at the Ryde end of the train, and boys at the Ventnor end, and there was strictly no fraternising, until, that is, the rarefied heights of the fifth were reached, when apparently sexual behaviour could be controlled in a more adult way.....

As far as discipline and school image was concerned, the school trains might have been run by the Sandown Grammar School Board of Governors, and were, simply, an extension of the school. Bear in mind that the coaches of the Island trains were all compartment stock, and that the trains used by the school children were also normal scheduled services. The "image" of the school (although this was not a fashionable term then) was considered by the powers that be to be very important in the community.

Image or no, in compartments uncluttered by members of the general public, there was always an opportunity for may-

hem, or even minor bullying. The favourite game amongst the boys was "Train He", which had rather different rules from the conventional game of "He" (or "Touch"). The game was, of course, limited to one compartment. The person who was "He" was blindfolded (usually with a school scarf) and had to fumble his way around the compartment, endeavouring to catch another player, who then had to be identified. If the identification was correct, the blindfold was passed to the individual caught, and so on. There was no limit to the territory in the compartment, so most Sandown Grammar boys who travelled by train became adept at climbing on luggage racks, squeezing into impossible corners between window and roof, and rolling under seats, as well as leaping gazelle-like around the limited space to avoid the outstretched arms of "He". Very occasionally, there was a broken window to be paid for.

Minor victimisation or punishment was not unknown, and most boys spent several journeys of their school lives on the luggage rack or under the seat at the dictates of their fellows, or even, let it be said, of the train prefect. From time to time some were to be observed leaving the train late at Ventnor, stopping to re-thread shoelaces which had been removed and tied in complex knots around the communication cord. All these activities took on a particularly sharp edge when a member of the public entered the compartment without warning at an intermediate stop!

What the girls got up to was largely a mystery, which even my sister, when she joined Sandown a year later, would shed no light upon!

A major train crime was leaning out of an open window. To be caught doing this was met by severe censure. Leaning out of the window, however, carried particular spice because of a curiosity of juvenile logic. To be caught not wearing school cap (or beret for the girls) was definitely one the most heinous of offences. This meant that all save a few

who were beyond the behavioural pale went everywhere during the journeys to and from school with their headgear almost glued to their heads. Because of this, if leaning out of the carriage window took place, inevitably the hat was being worn. If the hat was then blown away in the slipstream, since another avidly applied school rule was that all garments should be tagged with their owner's names, this meant that return of caps and berets automatically proved the guilt of the wearers. And the Station Master at Sandown - a man not unlike the late King George VI to look at - was continually and, we felt, gleefully, returning hats which had been picked up at the lineside by platelayers or permanent way gangs to the school office, with the inevitable result. The young travellers could have made life so much easier for themselves by just removing cap or beret before attempting to get an eye full of cinders from the locomotive!

One place where leaning out of the window took on a completely different dimension for a time was at Wroxall, where the 4.26 from Sandown crossed the 4.40pm from Ventnor. A long-suffering primary school teacher from Ventnor whose name was Irons always returned to his home at Shanklin on the latter train. Many of the Ventnor bound boys had been taught by him before their Grammar School life, and they, with the pathetic humour of the young teenager, felt in honour bound to lean out of the window and offer various versions of "Any Old Iron?". Occasionally, the teacher responded with anger, and, of course, this only spurred the boys on to greater efforts on the following days. Once, however, Mr Irons had his own back. A boy, particularly keen to demonstrate his lack of fear to his friends, a boy, moreover, who was a newcomer to the Island and who had never been taught by Mr Irons or been to his school, leaned out of the window to face the other train at Wroxall, and gave vent to a stentorian cry of "Any Old Iron?". In a flash, the window of the compartment of the Shanklin bound train opposite was dropped open, and a furious Mr Irons thrust his face close to that of the boy and hissed "Yes? What do you want?" The boy, too callow even to say "Good Evening", was nonplussed and embarrassed, withdrawing in a blushing heap into his compartment, and sagging into his seat. Both trains proceeded on their respective journeys. The boy's daring cut no ice, and even dented his reputation. His new-found friends only laughed. He never shouted out of the train window at Wroxall again.

No. 28 'Ashey' at Sandown with a Ventnor train. 14 June 1958.

ENTRANCE
TO
STATION.

3

Gently the daily usage of the train from Ventnor to Sandown became a routine. I ceased to look out of the window for the whole journey, and found other things to occupy the time. It has to be admitted that the twenty minutes or so of the journey were a heaven-sent opportunity for completion of homework or lines set as punishment. Routine it might have been, but total immersion gave insight into how the system worked, and an eye for detail recorded numerous things, unimportant at the time, but now, perhaps, worth recalling.

Ventnor station early in the morning acted like a magnet, drawing a horde of blue-clad school children into its interior. Sometimes the school train had not arrived, and knots of satchel-swinging youngsters spread themselves along the platform to bag the best seats when it appeared. In those days the station boasted both refreshment room and bookstall, and these were used on occasions by those with pocket-money to spare. There was an air of bustle about, almost akin to the Southern on the mainland.

The outside of the station was graced by a splendid Victorian hexagonal letterbox with the vertical slot, passed daily, and taken for granted, and the sign above the entrance still announced "Southern Railway". Inside, the platforms seemed spacious, with the curiosity of the custom-built gangway used to bridge the gap between the main platform one and the island platform two. To juvenile eyes the existence of a platform on each side of one track was an oddity, and I used to idly wonder what would happen if a passenger alighted from the wrong side of the train and found themselves marooned on the island platform. There were tubs of hydrangeas - a particularly Isle of Wight shrub - and the whole place seemed spick-and-span.

I think there was only one occasion a day during the winter when Platform Two was regularly used, and that was for the "school train" - the 4.52pm arrival.

The goods yard was spacious, and in a number of ways unique. It was entered by means of a road off the forecourt of the station which crossed the very end of the engine release road, whose buffer-stop was right against the wall of the cutting (I didn't realise until many years afterwards that the release road had replaced a Bembridge-style turntable in early Southern Railway days). The track layout in the yard boasted not one, but two, double-slips, both worked by hand levers (some latterly published track diagrams of the station

are wrong, and don't show the correct siding layout). The "back wall" of the goods yard had a number of man-made caves which were used as stores. I clearly remember that one had "ARP Shelter" inscribed over it in whitewash - quaint at this distance in time, but then we were less than ten years from VE-Day. The proximity of the radar installation on St Boniface Down, with its attraction for enemy aircraft, must have meant that the shelter was a useful asset in its day.

Scattered around the goods yard were usually half-a-dozen or so wagons supplying the local coal merchants. Other types were rare. At this time, coal was practically the only surviving revenue-earning freight that the system carried.

Between the run-round loop and the goods yard was a rolling stock siding, which contained spare coaches laid-up for the winter. Between them and the buffer-stop, adjacent to the water-crane serving the run-round loop, was always a coal wagon or two, presumably with emergency loco supplies, although I never saw them used. The train we caught every Monday morning was, during the winter, a standard three-coach set, and the locomotive collected a further coach from the stock siding to attach to the front of the train. Frequently it seemed as if this extra coach was relatively newly out-shopped, and was in good condition. I am perfectly certain that on one occasion at least one bogie was fitted with Mansell wheels - I can see the wooden segments as clearly now as if it was yesterday.

The tunnel mouth was never without its wisp of smoke, clearing from the passage of the last train, and the signalbox always looked cosy, with its convenient balcony for tablet exchange.

At the Ryde end of the platform was a bay which terminated in a huge, dark, always empty goods shed, and from this road was another short siding, terminating behind the signalbox, whose sole use seemed to be to store the tunnel inspection vehicle - a simple device consisting of a raised wooden platform mounted on a platelayer's trolley.

The dank journey through the tunnel seemed to take an inordinate time, and one always seemed to emerge into a different world at the other end. A short burst of daylight and fields, and then Wroxall, with its ivy-clad hotel and signal box in the main station building. Beyond the bridge was the solitary, seldom-used siding, opposite Flux's bacon factory, which was busy in those days, and once had a siding of its

Opposite - No. 16 'Ventnor' storming up Apse bank, past the Shanklin up distant, with a train for Ventnor. 28 June 1958.

No. 28 'Ashey' at Sandown with a Ventnor train. 14 June 1958.

own. I don't know exactly when the latter was lifted, but signs of it were clearly visible at this time.

Our Monday morning train from Ventnor used to cross with the freight working from Newport at Wroxall. Usually this consisted of one of the E1's heading a handful of loaded coal wagons, and a brake van, although occasionally other items would appear, such as a ten-tonner full of ashes from either Ryde or Newport shed. Whatever Ventnor wanted these for, I can't guess. On another occasion an otherwise completely empty open wagon contained a one of the gangways used to

board the ferries at Ryde Pier Head, and this joined and eventually superseded the custom-built specimen used for bridging the gap between the platforms at Ventnor. I think it stayed there until the bitter end.

The journeys, even the longer trips to mainland destinations, became sunk in normality. Arrival at Ventnor, though, was always an important event, with a passengers gathering themselves together, heading for the exit and meeting love-ones, and a good deal of important activity involving station staff and guard, with trolleys and packages and mail sacks, and the impatient panting of the Westinghouse pump on the engine. Then, as things quietened, there would be the clang of uncoupling, and with a scarcely audible puff the locomotive would pull gently forward, over the points on to the release road, and then quietly back to the water-crane for replenishment.

Always an awesome location physically, Ventnor station took on an even more wild atmosphere in the depths of winter storms. Leaving the warmth of the train was one thing, but turning your back on the comforting lights of the station and heading up the dimly lit road for the three-quarter mile walk home was another, and somehow seemed a slightly dangerous thing to do, with more than a touch of the demonic about it. Time and again, when the weather was bad

and you could hear the sea pounding the rocks three hundred feet below, and the wind was cold in your teeth and took your breath away, I thought of the lines from "The "Immortal Hour" which had lodged in my mind, quoted by Hamilton Ellis in his book "The Trains We Loved", of which I had a much-read copy…

*"You have come but a little way, who think so far
The long uncounted leagues to the world's end!"*

Hamilton Ellis used them to describe Owencarrow on the Londonderry and Lough Swilly's remote extension to Burtonport, but I found the dark winter reaches of Ventnor just as supernatural....

An interesting view of an unidentified O2 bringing a train from Cowes up the 1 in 55 gradient into Sandown from the direction of Alverstone and Merstone. The first two coaches appear to be ex-LCDR bogies, and these, together with the locomotive livery, probably date the photograph to the summer of 1949.

Paul Hersey collection

On what appears to be a less than warm spring day, No. 28 'Ashey' taking water at Ventnor after arrival of a train from Ryde. 17 April 1960.

No. 36 'Carisbrooke' arriving at Shanklin with a train for Ventnor. 23 May 1959.

The cold of winter turned into the spring of 1955, precursor of a long, hot summer.

Travels by train there were, but few details stay in the mind. The Island railways were observed from afar, also - a particularly easy thing to do when so much rolling downland gave the opportunity for aerial views. We spent much time sitting in the sun near the obelisk at the top of the steep slope where Stenbury Down fell away towards Godshill and Wroxall. From here there was an uninterrupted view across the centre of the Island, and with the countryside laid out before the eye like a marvellously coloured map one could trace the passage of trains over the whole length of the Sandown-Newport line from Alverstone to Blackwater. Little slow-moving worms with a plume of steam at their head worked their way across the tapestry of fields, taken largely for granted by the onlooker, oblivious to the fact that this was to be the last summer that they would ever be seen.

Ventnor, so it seemed, was not to be the family's final resting place. Came the late summer of 1955, and moving was again on the agenda. We took up residence at Shanklin in the autumn. Aside from a new home, life didn't change very much. I still caught the same trains to and from school.

Perhaps now is a good time to mention the curious business of distances on Islands. There is some odd law of space and time which dictates that miles lengthen in small, physically isolated places. Ventnor is as different from Ryde as chalk from cheese, yet the two are separated by a mere dozen miles. Newport is around ten miles from Shanklin, but when I was young a visit there was considered to be something that took up a whole day. Even now, when I work on the Island from time to time, I am still amazed by the time it takes to drive from the ferry at Yarmouth to Newport - a distance that would occupy only minutes on the mainland. (Oddly, this lengthening miles business is not confined to Wight: I notice it, too, in the Channel Islands, and I'm sure it must be so in other offshore places.)

It was no wonder, then, that the journey from home at Shanklin to school at Sandown seemed a distance to be reckoned with, although it was only three miles. A walk or bus trip into town (with a walk from the bus station) brought us to the railway station, where we travelled for one stop on the train, with the whole rigmarole repeated vice versa at the end of the day, and the journeys occupying around three quarters of an hour! At the time, however, it was the most natural thing in the world.

Most of my impressions of Shanklin station had been formed before taking residence on the Island. During my time commuting from Ventnor it had simply been a place where others joined or left the train, but now I had the chance to study it once more.

Like all Island stations at that time, Shanklin had its fair share of interest. Two booking-office windows (only one of which seemed ever to be open) looked out on a slightly dim booking hall with echoing floorboards. Opposite the booking office was W.H.Smith's bookstall, and the entrance to the platform was guarded by the ticket collector's cubbyhole. Adjacent to this (as with a number of other Island stations) was a splendid platform ticket machine which looked old-fashioned even then. Access from the down to the up platform was achieved by the dank subway - the Isle of Wight Railway seemed to prefer this method of moving people from one platform to another. There was a signalbox high above the up platform just as at Sandown, though less obvious, from which the signalman had to descend to exchange the single-line tokens with engine crews.

At this time Shanklin Gasworks was still operating. It was served by a short siding which trailed off the up loop, and there always seemed to be a wagon or two being emptied of coal. This must have been a back- breaking job of the kind that has nowadays, thankfully, almost disappeared. One or two men stood inside the wagon being emptied, and shovelled the coal onto a chute which deposited it in the gasworks, the plant being below the level of the railway. When a new plant to serve the whole Island opened south of East Cowes, I think in 1957, with supplies brought in by sea, the existing works became storage places only, and with the demise of those at Ryde and Shanklin as rail-served gas producers, another nail was knocked into the coffin of the Island railway's freight traffic.

At the Ryde end of the down platform was the short bay, which in the summer frequently used to unload a utility or other van or two full of scouts or other parties' camping gear sent in advance of their arrival. The solitary siding in the goods yard, accessed from the head-shunt, seldom held any rolling stock save wagons with coal merchants' supplies.

Sandown station always seemed large and spacious, although with the passing years I find that it has shrunk somewhat. I suppose during school time I tended to regard it as merely as a staging post, although it had its fair share of interest. One of the items which continually occupied a number of us was a machine for stamping out name tags on strips of aluminium. These were somewhat like huge, primeval Dymo tape machines, and were once commonplace. Now, doubtless, they are valuable museum pieces. I think the investor was allowed 21 letters, numbers, symbols or spaces for one penny, but I regret to say that some of us discovered how to make the slide mechanism which took the coins work without the use of cash, and from time to time we extracted enormous lengths of aluminium strip which became important, but totally useless, trophies!

The waiting room was spacious, with Southern benches and a warm fire in the winter. Adorning the wall, behind glass, was a relief model of the Island with the railways clearly marked.

Particularly when the Sandown-Newport line was open, Sandown was a busy place, even in the winter. There were a couple of freight workings every day, and though there was little save a handful of coal wagons, full to be positioned in the sidings, and empties to be disposed of, the engines of the freight trains - E1's during my early acquaintance - seemed to linger a long while.

The school train to and from Newport was a special working, and the train engine was more often than not an E1. Having disgorged their load of children, the three coaches were parked on the stock siding adjacent to the platform three run round loop until they were required for the return trip in the afternoon. After disposing of them in the morning, the locomotive returned light to Newport, to reappear around 3.30pm to take the train away.

Although the curve of the Newport line as it approached Sandown was on a stiff-ish gradient, it was the habit of train crews to coast the final couple of hundred yards. Whether the closing of the regulator caused peculiarities in the behaviour of the steam, I don't know, but I do remember on one occasion witnessing the locomotive give vent to a splendidly enormous smoke ring of exhaust which hung in the air for minutes.

The business of the railway was always a good measure of how time was going at school, and the sound (or sight, if one was in the right building or on the playing field) of trains was as good as a watch. The important fuss of a train approaching up the gradient from Brading, shutting off steam to coast into the station gave time a meaning, and frequently marked the end of forty minutes of tedious struggle with an unloved subject. On other occasions later in school days the sound of trains arriving or departing, clearly heard from the inside of the nearby Girl Guides' hut sequestered by the school during GCE examinations, could spell panic over unfinished work, or release from the certain knowledge of failure. Likewise, in those earlier days, the arrival of the light engine from Newport meant that only twenty minutes or so of the day remained. Cold on a winter playing field, talentless amongst the skill of others, the sight was welcome: less so in the warm and interesting woodwork room when things were going well.

Mention of the woodwork room calls to mind the teacher responsible for trying to instil the rudiments of carpentry. He was undoubtedly one of the nicest people in the world, and this niceness was even further enhanced by his liking for railways. A native Islander, he (with another master) looked after the school's Railway Club, and, when the time was right, could be persuaded to tell tales of his own school journeys on the train, which I suspect were in late Isle of

Last months of decay on the Sandown - Newport line. The track between Sandown and Alverstone, looking towards Sandown. 4 August 1959.

Demolition of the Newport line at Sandown. 17 April 1960.

Wight Central or early Southern days.

About eighteen months after the closure of the Sandown-Newport line, an O2 with a string of empty wagons, the Ryde breakdown crane and a brake van, ventured down the line from Sandown to collect little concrete platelayers' shelters from the lineside for use elsewhere. From later evidence of disturbed rust on the tracks, I think the ensemble reached somewhere around Horringford. The woodwork room ground to a halt whilst the teacher and a few properly-minded pupils dashed to the window to observe the progress of the train.

By the time we moved to Shanklin, the fate of the Sandown-Newport line was pretty much decided, the apparent charade of the public enquiry not altering things one jot. The County Council's Education Department did its best, so I was later informed, to boost passenger numbers by insisting that pupils transferred to Sandown Grammar when Cowes Technical School closed in 1955, travelled from East Cowes by the chain ferry, and then onwards to Sandown by train from Mill Hill. Sadly, this effort didn't change things, and the end came in February 1956.

When the time for the Sandown-Newport line's closure arrived, we were well ensconced in Shanklin, and I should, by rights have been present at its decease. My appetite for wakes, though, has never been good, and I stayed away. To

have been there would, I fear, have hurt too much.

On the Monday following the closure, three buses arrived at the school with the former Newport and Cowes line travellers, and appeared again to collect them at the end of the day. Thus was the transition made, smoothly and efficiently, and the only noticeable change was the transit time of the travellers. There may have been regrets amongst those who travelled, but they weren't voiced loudly, although the History master - a relatively new arrival at the school who used to travel on the train from Blackwater - made one or two comments which seemed to me to indicate that he was not unmoved. Certainly, as part of his introduction to local history for the first-formers the Isle of Wight's Railways featured prominently, so perhaps they meant more to him than to many.

Sandown station became an emptier place, the IWCR sidings were emptied of rolling stock, including the train of ballast wagons which appeared at closure where the coaches for the school train to Newport used to be stored during the day, and the lines rusted and gradually became immersed in mares-tails.

One of the curiosities of Sandown Grammar School during my tenure was that it had a split site. Having hopelessly outgrown the original turn-of-the-century building on the east of the railway, new accommodation, eventually to

Demolition of the Newport line at Sandown. New platform 3 arrangement with wagons 60562, ex-LSWR Road Vehicle Truck (nearest camera), and DS46957, an ex-LBSCR 10-ton van. 17 April 1960.

house the whole school, had been built on another site a half a mile to the west. During my time, science and workshop facilities, and all catering was on the new campus, and this meant that almost every child in the school had to cross the railway to and from their school dinner. Even though the school was small by modern standards, this daily expedition by around three to four hundred children needed to be well organised. There was a lane which led past the station fore-court to an occupation crossing (called, I think, Cox's Cross-ing), designated as a private road, and protected by locked gates on either side. Pedestrian access was normally gained by using small gates at the edge of the road, but these would have been hopelessly inadequate for coping with the num-bers, so in advance of the phalanx of children a member of

staff would proceed to the station booking office to collect the keys for the padlocks on the road gates. No child, ex-cept sixth-formers, was allowed to use the crossing until the main gates were open, and the member of staff was always present to ensure safe passage.

Once the horde was safely across, with the teacher watching their progress, the gates would be re-locked until the whole process was repeated in reverse after lunch, and the keys duly returned to the booking office. It was all pretty safe, really, because train times and the school dinner break did not (by design, I imagine) coincide.

At other times of the day children moving between sites, or the playing fields between them, made their own way across the tracks, unguarded and unsupervised. I seem to remember that the School Governors fussed about the safety of this from time to time, but I cannot recall a single instance of stupidity on the part of the youthful users of the crossing. To be sure, it was tempting, in spite of the large notices of prohibition and potential traps of signal cables and point rodding, to gain direct access to the station platforms by way of their end ramps adjacent to the crossing when one finished the day at the school site to the west of the railway. The official route was the walking of the two sides of the triangle using the lane and crossing the station forecourt.

The temptation of the short-cut was seldom succumbed to, and if deviation from the rules was detected there was a certain detention at the end of the excursion.

The daily school rail journey gave an intimacy with its route that did not apply to other parts of the system. Knowledge of these came by way of different travel objectives - usually, for a teenager, social and pleasure, but sometimes as a result of parental business or school trips. If lack of intimacy denied familiarity with some of the everyday quirks of operation, depth of interest in the subject still enabled the painting of an interesting canvas over the years.

Above - *Ex-LBSCR 10-ton crane (D426) with match-truck (DS3138) at Brickfield Sidings, Sandown. 8 August 1959.*

Right - *Chock to stop runaways on the Newport line stock siding at Sandown. 17 April 1960.*

No 25 'Godshill' coaling at Ryde. 11 October 1958.

It was always reassuring - in the way of things not changing - to see the remains of the Bembridge line curving away from Brading. The signalman still crossed the track from his remote box at Brading to exchange tablets with train crews on the Ryde-Ventnor line, sometimes the rust on the rails towards Bembridge looked just a little newer, and oblivion, although possible, seemed largely out of sight. There was an inevitability that the track would be taken up eventually, but as month succeeded month and the years turned and it still survived, one felt that some of the rumours of take-over of the Island's railways, or at least the closed ones, by this or that organisation which were heard again and again might just hold a little water.

The family visited St. Helens and Bembridge one day in April 1957 by bus from Ryde. I was looking forward to seeing St. Helen's Quay again, and this time, with my added maturity since my discovery of the place in 1949, to examining the track layout if nothing else. What I was not prepared for was the presence of rolling stock, and great was my delight when approaching down a side road to see a coach, disused with broken windows, parked on one of the sidings. Double delight, because the vehicle was still in Southern Railway green. More delight than ever to find other sidings full of coaching stock and wagons. Slightly diminished delight to discover that this was in many respects a grave yard, and that coaches were being demolished.

How I wish that I had had the sense to record in detail the things that were there instead of just wandering amongst the hulks and the disarray, for here was possibly one of the last chances to connect with some of the railway items of earlier times. I remember noticing that the curious siding which crossed the Embankment Road had been removed, but that nothing else save the wheeled vehicles had been touched. I did map the layout, and I suppose that at least was something.

The day of reckoning was not long delayed, and the tracks were lifted from Brading to Bembridge in April 1958. Around that time the vicinity of Ryde works was filled with down-at-heel wagons covered with "Not To Go" and "For Repair" notices. Some of their timbers were green with neglect, and I supposed that they had been rescued from the final destruction at St. Helens. The turntable well at Bembridge was filled in, and memories of the railway rapidly disappeared, aided by the fact that the demolition of the line had been done by road vehicles.

The signalbox at Brading now seemed even more remote, but the station, if not busy in itself, still played its part in the busy schedule of the summer timetable. Chalk siding to the south of the station was seldom empty, and its extremity was occupied for a long time from early 1958 by the half-converted ex-LBSC saloon coach which eventually became the Ryde breakdown van. This conversion, incidentally, must be one of the longest on record, the time taken being more than two years from start to finish. Perhaps it was a low priority "fill-in" for Ryde Works when nothing more important was going on. I got the impression from one or two who worked there that they were not over-enamoured with the decision to spend scarce money on an item which might never be used, especially when there was a perfectly good, if somewhat unkempt, existing breakdown van, itself converted from an ex-LSWR four-wheeler. The new vehicle spent a lot of its early conversion time on Chalk Siding, presumably to make room for other activities at Ryde.

Smallbrook Junction, remote and open for only a few months of the year, was a good indicator of the passing seasons. During the winter, the trains from Newport and Ventnor galloped by on their respective tracks, heedless of the tiny signal cabin and the bare signal posts. Then in the late spring, signal arms would appear, with crosses attached to them to show that they meant nothing as yet. And then the official pronouncement that summer had arrived. Smallbrook became a proper junction, the start of double track towards Ryde; trains crossed tracks and the signalman collected and handed out tokens as they passed. Then at the dismal end of summer, the mid-September dismembering of signals and the shut down until the sun came back meant that once again, for a few months, we largely had our Island to ourselves.

Ryde St. Johns Road was not the true hub of the system, of course. Geographically, this had always been Newport, and still should have been but for the closures. Nevertheless, much that was interesting and tasty was here, and it was a place that continually gave interest. Amongst other things, as I became older and history was meaning more, I found pleasure in the discovery that the platform awning supports sported the IWR monogram. Most times, the view of St. Johns was from a train either to or from the Pier Head, but the station stop always allowed the shed and works to be seen, and I also put in an increasing number of visits especially to see what was happening.

The Works was one of those places where you knew things were going on, but where there was little obvious activity.

Left - *The little ex-IWCR crane, No. 425S, built by Kirkstall Forge in 1865*, outside Ryde Works. 27 August 1958. This was one of Mike Jacobs' favourite items of Island rolling stock, and is now happily preserved in Leeds by the successors to its makers. (* - a build date 1864 has also been suggested.)*
Right - *No. 27 'Merstone' undergoing repairs in Ryde Works. 27 August 1958.*

It wasn't exactly sleepy-hollow, but there were never armies of men doing things, at least not in the visible area outside. Usually a locomotive was under the sheer-legs, perhaps minus a pair of driving wheels; usually a carriage, newly painted, was jacked up at one end waiting for a bogie; usually there were wagons awaiting seeing to, or occasionally containing spare parts or pieces of timber. Sometimes the boiler wagon would be there with a new boiler, painted in red oxide ready to be fitted to whichever locomotive was inside the Works. Always visible was the little four-wheeled IWR two-ton crane, which I never saw used, but which was never in the same position twice, and which enjoyed a complete repaint in 1958.

The service vehicles, after the manner of their kind, because of their infrequent hard work, were mostly interesting relics of former times. The boiler wagon was a conversion from an IWR carriage truck and looked its age. In the days of St. Helens Quay it made forays there from time to time with boilers for refurbishment at Eastleigh and to collect new boilers delivered from the mainland, but after complete closure of that line its sole running as far as my observations went, save for a trip to Sandown to get it out of the way for the summer of 1958, was from the goods yard at Ryde St, Johns, where it would be loaded with a boiler brought to the Island by road, across to the Works where the boiler would be unloaded for use in locomotive overhaul. Loading and unloading in the goods yard was done by the ex-LBSC ten-ton crane - the mainstay of the Island's breakdown fleet, although seldom in my time called upon to serve in that capacity - which otherwise tended to live permanently on the stores siding between the Motive Power Depot and the Sta-

tion. It did get out once in a while, on trips such as the hut collecting run to Horringford already mentioned, and it did spend time on Chalk Siding at Brading and, like the boiler wagon, also at Sandown, to get it out of the way during the summer. This crane, of the heaviest capacity on the Island, had a proper match truck. There was one other crane, too, which I only ever saw at Newport, and which scarcely moved during its final British Railways years. This was the ex-MR six-wheeler, originally discovered in the closed emptiness of Newport Shed in 1958 without a match truck. This state of affairs had been rectified by the next year, when it had acquired, or reacquired, obviously not in the same Siamese-twin way as the ten-ton crane, an ex-LSW wagon as a mate. Happily, this pair eventually found their way to the preserved Isle of Wight Steam Railway at Haven Street.

I managed a number of visits to Ryde Works during the late fifties and early sixties. Only one of these, the first in 1958, was almost legal. I had written to British Railways seeking formal permission for myself and a friend to visit both Ryde Motive Power Depot and Ryde Works. Back came the reply from Waterloo with an official form allowing us access to the MPD, but with a note appended informing us that there was no works at Ryde! Perhaps they knew it as something different, but to us it seemed more like a railway works than anything else. After all, complete overhauls of locomotives and rolling stock were carried out there, and the only thing that they couldn't do was heavy casting or boiler refurbishment.

Anyhow, call it what they liked, we still gained access, and very interesting it was, too. In the locomotive works No. 27

Withdrawn No. 4 'Wroxall' languishes at the end of the coal stage supply siding at Ryde shed. 19 May 1961.

was receiving attention, and the carriage and wagon part of the building was hosting, amongst other items, the partly converted new breakdown van. We were shown around by a gentleman who I think was the Works Foreman, reinforced by his wearing of a hat rather than the caps sported by other lowlier grades. Using that initial visit as a kind of passport, entry to the Works became easier. The foreman said "If you want to visit again, don't go to the entrance on St John's Road. Shout across from platform three to one of the men, and ask if I'm around. I'll come and get you from the platform." I gathered he thought that the official gatekeeper was somewhat of what is nowadays called a "jobsworth", who was inclined to be obstructive. Using the suggested method several subsequent trips around the small facility were made.

The Southern had spent a lot on money and energy rationalising the facilities at Ryde St. Johns, the products of which have been recorded many times elsewhere, and even in the late fifties there was still a tangible atmosphere of "Southern-ness" about the place. The MPD was always neat and tidy, the locomotives got cleaned (at least until nearly the end), and that was miracle enough on British Railways in the fifties and sixties. Of course, during daily summer operation, particularly on Saturdays, the place would be all but empty, but during the low season there was little room to spare.

Newport Shed closed in November 1957, and its complement of locomotives went to Ryde. The numbers had already diminished slightly, four of the O2's and two of the E1's having been scrapped earlier, and I can remember 19 and 23 awaiting their fate on the stores siding at Ryde in 1956. Even after this reduction in numbers, however, Ryde Shed had still technically to house twenty-one engines, and this was clearly a difficult task. The problem was solved to some extent by lodging rows of dead locomotives on the stores siding or number one locomotive road (the siding which served the coaling stage), but pressure on space in the winter caused four engines to be domiciled for the winter of 1957/58 in the disused Newport Shed. The next two winters also saw four locomotives hibernate, this time out of doors at Sandown's Brickfield Sidings.

The coaling arrangements at Ryde seemed to me to encourage backbreaking work. Whilst the wagons which brought the coal could be discharged on to the stage at floor level, the tops of the bunkers of the O2's were higher than this, and so all supplies had to be lifted into them with a shovel. With an early notion of work-study, I was contemplating this problem during a 1961 visit to the shed, when all thoughts of the problems of coal handling were put out of my mind by the discovery of the last E1, No 4, long withdrawn, but still largely intact, lodged at the end of the number one road.

Above - Ex-MR 6-wheeled crane inside the disused loco shed at Newport. 20 May 1961.

Left - Boiler wagon (ex-IWR carriage truck) DS349 at Ryde with a replacement boiler for No. 26. 14 April 1959.

Opposite page - No. 3 'Ryde' being dismantled at Ryde MPD. 29 August 1959.

The late summer of 1959 was a time of almost weekly journeys to the mainland, set aside other parts of the Island, and trip by trip, I watched the slow demise of No 3 as she was cut up in the stores siding. It was a curious thing that as parts of her anatomy were removed, she took on more and more the appearance of an antediluvian locomotive. And then suddenly she wasn't there anymore, only a pile of anonymous scrap whose disappearance coincided with my own disappearance as an Island resident.

Ryde Esplanade was not a station that I got to know very well, in spite of having friends at Ryde and travelling regularly for a few weeks to visit a girlfriend there. That it was spacious and busy there was no doubt, but I suspect that it does not stick too readily in my mind because it was only a place that trains stopped at on their way to stations of more interest. No sidings and no signalbox meant no quirks, although the saving grace was, of course, the southern terminus of the Pier Tramway. Like many other things at the time, the tramway was taken for granted, and I can remember that the only outstanding contribution it made to my

interest in railways was when one of the passenger cars appeared in Southern green in 1956, a little while before the official announcement of the BR livery changes that year, which brought the Island a little closer to my original memories. I remember wondering if the Island had declared a colourful unilateral declaration of independence (although we wouldn't have called it that in those days) from the overall monotony of BR, and this view was reinforced only days later by the appearance of a newly out-shopped ex-SEC full brake conversion also in the lovely green. Then an item on liveries appeared in the newspapers and the change was confirmed as official. The march back to the old order began, although it took quite six years to accomplish.

There was again much "Southern-ness" at Ryde Pier Head, unique station where there were always many people passing to and from the ferries, greeted on their arrival as the ferry tied up by a lovely welcoming announcement in a calm and slightly local voice over the public address. As I recall, it went something like this: "Good morning (or afternoon, or evening) ladies and gentlemen. Welcome to the Isle of

Busy times at Ryde Pier Head with a train for Ventnor departing from Platform 1. Summer 1949.   *Denis Callender*

Wight. Passengers for Ryde should proceed.....” and so on, with guidance for those travelling to all destinations. We would call it "customer care" nowadays, but a nicer entry to the Island, even for regular travellers, would have been hard to conceive.

Little Lister tractors were constantly buzzing around and in and out of the Pier Head station like busy insects, transporting luggage trailers between boat and train. These luggage trailers, three-wheeled and stoutly built, were used for the transhipment of luggage and parcels from train to boat at Portsmouth and Ryde. They were loaded on to the ferry at one end by electric crane, off at the other by the same method, and towed by the Lister tractors to the luggage accommodation on the trains. Some writers have said that, like the later BRUTES elsewhere, they were transported on the Island's trains and put off at appropriate stations, but I never saw this happen, and don't think it did during my time. Oddly enough, though, I used to wonder why it wasn't done, particularly in the summer, because it would have cut station time quite considerably.

There was always a wait for the trains to depart from the Pier Head. This gave ample, if sometimes slightly boring, opportunity to inspect the insides of the compartments.

The discerning traveller soon came to know that the interiors of the ex-SECR coaches were very much more comfortable than those of the ex-LBSCR. The former had interior-sprung cushions, whilst the seats in the latter were merely upholstered benches, albeit with springs. There was a rather more spartan approach all round with the Brighton specimens, which were further distinguished by their door-handles and locking mechanisms. The handles on the Brighton fleet were larger than those on the Chatham vehicles, and once shut could only be opened from the inside by lowering the window and turning the handle. The first movement of the handle was to around forty-five degrees, and then only by further movement against a spring could the

door be opened. This system gave station staff and guards an immediate indication that a door was not properly closed, and the sound of handles being turned to the horizontal was always a prelude to movement out of a station. The Chatham species of door lock was much more modern, resembling the locks still in use until relatively recently on British Rail slam door multiple units.

The inside of present day railway vehicles is a world away from the compartment stock that I grew up with on the Island, and the curves, the joinery, the drop-lights with their leather straps, and the photographs or reproduction water-colours above the seats belonged to another age. One youthful discovery was that in the ex-LBSC coaches, using a pen-knife as a screwdriver to remove the wooden frames of the photographs or prints enabled one to reverse the cardboard mounts, and when the whole was reassembled the slogan "Places of Interest on the London, Brighton & South Coast Railway" once more took its place over the backs of the seats as in days of yore! It might seem odd to succeeding generations that we never even contemplated stealing these trophies, although they must have been worth having as curios even then.

Because it was our transit station for the mainland, we chiefly saw Ryde Pier Head at the beginnings and ends of days. Daytime memories seem always to be of summer morning sunlight, prior to a faintly hazy crossing with the mirror-like sea incredibly quiet and still, the way only the Solent behaves sometimes. It wasn't always like this, though - I can remember a crossing on midsummer's day, I think in 1958, when the sea was so rough that the ferry shipped water at the bow, from whence much of it ran all the way down the deck to return to the sea over the stern! Evening memories seem to centre more on winter. A breezy crossing, followed by the womb of the carriage compartment, warm and dimly lit, with the locomotive taking water from the tank at the landward end of platform one. A feel-

No. 17 'Seaview' passing the disused Ryde Gasworks with a Ventnor train. Although buried, the sidings are still in situ. 27 August 1958.

ing that, interesting though the day may have been, shopping in Portsmouth or a making a trip to London, we were back in our own place.

Then the journey. The gentle gait of the train down the Pier, the rapidly accelerating descent from Ryde Esplanade, the fiery shadows of the gasworks (before it closed), sleepy St. Johns, with dim light emerging from the shed, and then off into the countryside. Brave exhaust beats to Smallbrook and on to Brading. Pause and quiet, broken only by the beat of the Westinghouse pump and a railway voice calling out "Brading, Brading" and then more quiet. Brading seemed to be the only place where the station name was shouted. I remember on one trip the post-"Brading, Brading" silence being broken by the window of the next compartment being

opened, and one of several youths within shouting to the porter "Yes?". The porter courteously enquired what was amiss, and the youth replied "I thought you wanted me. My name's Brading! Is this the last train to San Fernando?" Immense hilarity from next door....

The silence broken by the locomotive's whistle, and a sharp getaway as a preamble to the pull up the bank and a businesslike entry to Sandown. Then onward and upward over Lake bridge, rattling along in fine style, through more lights, more habitation, to alight at Shanklin. The walk home from the station accompanied to begin with by the shouting of the locomotive starting its ascent of the long Apse Bank, and then, eventually, silence, broken only by the sound of our footsteps.

No. 32 'Bonchurch' having just departed from Brading with a Ventnor train. 25 July 1959.

6

As the fifties progressed, so my maturing approach to the world enabled me to think beyond the immediate and obvious railway things, and I took an increasing interest in historical and less obvious railway angles, sparked off, I think, by the discovery in 1956 of Michael Robbins' excellent little book "The Isle of Wight Railways", published by the Oakwood Press. Reading this introduced me properly to the wonderfully varied background of the Island's lines, and created a desire for more intimate knowledge of their history. I had no knowledge of how to undertake historical research, but the fundamentals of delving into the past came easily, particularly when I discovered the pleasure of making facts fit like a jigsaw, or turning up something that seemed really brand new, or finding evidence which, in a way, put me ahead of some of the "experts".

Thus it was that abiding memories of a two week visit to hospital in late 1956 revolve around listening to tales from the other side of the ward of problems encountered by hauliers on some part of Medina Wharf from the mouth of a man rather mangled in an accident involving a barge of some sort and a lorry, and hearing from an elderly Isle of Wight native in the bed next to me about his younger days travelling on the trains, and the fact that Lake Halt *did* exist. I felt that the latter rather put me one up on Michael Robbins, who mentioned it, but commented that he had no independent evidence of its existence!

The historical angles put me more in touch, too, with the minutiae of daily railway life, and made me pay attention to items that had not previously been thought worthy of notice. I discovered the innate interest that many everyday artifacts and activities involved with running the railways had, and started to observe the things around me with a keener eye for detail. Such things as axle boxes became an important

method of identifying the lineage of rolling stock - not infallible, but a useful guide. Rail chairs, previously overlooked as necessary, but boring, were seen in a new light, and told something of the past. Other items like signals, point rodding and station buildings and fittings became significant. An already rich diet of interest became richer, and thus icing, as it were, was added to my railway cake.

My burgeoning interest in delving manifested itself particularly in 1958 and 1959, when I began at last to understand that the economic sands of time seemed to be running out for the Island's remaining railways. So was my own life changing, and I knew that at the end of school life I would have little alternative but to pursue some kind of career away from the Island. These things pressed me to record and experience as much as I could whilst it was still possible and attainable.

I had a number of like-minded friends. In May 1958 we sought, and were granted, permission to walk the closed Sandown-Newport line. As part of the permission-seeking exercise, I visited the offices at Newport where the railway administration was still done, and was there interviewed by a kindly man who, in his later letter, signed himself as "S. Prismall". I didn't know at that time that he was a long-time railway servant on the Island, already working when Alastair McLeod took over the management in 1928, which was probably just as well; if I had, I would probably have pestered him with questions, and wasted his afternoon!

We set off to walk the line from Sandown on a warm Saturday in May. The track was still down, and little had really changed since the closure in 1956. There was no doubt, however, that closer acquaintance paid dividends of detail, and that one day enabled me to learn about the line in a way

Right - 1952 carriage notice.   *Denis Callender*

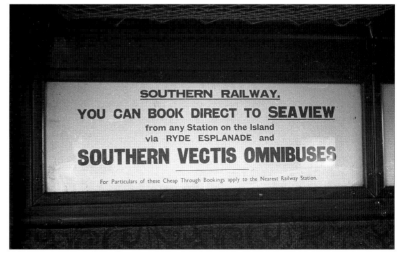

Left - *IWCR flat-bottom track spiked direct to sleepers, Pan Mill siding. 12 July 1958.*
Right - *IWR chair at Merstone.*   *Denis Callender*

which otherwise would have been impossible.

Rail chairs became the first observation of the day. A number of the chairs on the sidings were of IWR vintage - 1880 and 1882 were two of the years - and the very end of the short water crane road, used when the line was open, by locomotives replenishing supplies but not proceeding towards Ventnor, was of lightweight bullhead rail, held to the sleepers with spikes intended for the flat-bottomed variety. LSW pattern chairs were liberally scattered. These were of varying ages, and dated between 1873 and 1911. There was even one GWR example!

We examined the unusual "chock" used to prevent vehicles running away from the stock siding in the station, and discovered the flange-oiler installed on the curve into the station, and wondered if it was the only such device in the Island.

The signals on the Island had been modernised in early BR days, and we were used to the standard Southern upper-quadrant variety. It came as a pleasant surprise to find that the distants at Sandown and Shide (from the direction of Blackwater), though both fixed, were still of lower quadrant type.

It must not be imagined that we examined every inch of track, but chairs again occupied our observations. Very few were BR. Most were Southern of any date between 1925 and 1948; there was a good sprinkling of IWR types on sidings and there was one stretch - north of Merstone, as I recall - laid with a GKN patent track system. Slightly remarkable was a GWR example at Sandown and an S&DJR specimen near Alverstone, but most remarkable of all was Pan Mill Siding, not used for years before the last train on the "main line" ran, but still, however, in situ, though very overgrown. The first portion of this was bullhead rail laid on

SEC and - magic discovery - the only examples I ever discovered of IWC chairs. Even better was the fact that once clear of the pointwork, the siding was made of flat-bottomed rail, spiked directly to the sleepers, and this, I think, with the exception of lengths over the drawbridge at Newport, was the last remaining example of this style of track, once commonplace all over the Island.

We lunched in the signalbox at Merstone. There was no need to break in, vandals having done a thorough job on the whole station. The major fittings - the twenty-eight levers and the wheel for opening the level crossing - were still in place, but immovable. In the storage area at ground level were various bits and pieces, including a number of old train registers. I took one of these - it would only have decayed otherwise - as an historical record. Dated 1947, most pages, of course, simply recorded the daily run-of-the-mill signalling activities of this isolated rural junction, but occasionally there were intriguing entries such as "Ft to Horringford" and "Ft to Godshill", and I remember that one of the signalmen had the unusual name of Tosdevin. I kept the book for years until, fool that I was, I sold it for a pittance in a fit of pre-marital penury (that the marriage didn't work very well adds insult to injury!).

As part of the Island's contribution to musical revolution of the mid-fifties, there was a local skiffle group who called themselves "The Signal Box Five", who, so rumour had it, used the box at Merstone as a rehearsal room.

We finished the expedition by crossing Coppins Bridge and walking over the viaduct into Newport station. The station foreman took a somewhat dim view of this mode of entry into his territory, but he softened almost to obsequiousness when we explained that we "had permission from Mr Gardener" (who, I think, was called "Assistant for the Isle of

Merstone Station - much disused. 24 May 1958.

Wight" at this time - at any rate, he was in charge). Actually, I'm not sure that we did have permission, and I have a feeling that we should not have proceeded past Pan Lane crossing, but at any rate, the great man's name did the trick, and no further questions were asked.

At the time of our walk the line was still almost in one piece, save for a short stretch between Sandown and Alverstone where the railway had been removed to make way for a tracked crane to undertake work on the river bank (this piece was later re-laid, presumably by the crane's operators, but not very well), and the final lengths over the viaduct at Newport. New arrangements to the track and signalling there had not long been made, and there was now a single track exit from the station over the viaduct towards Ryde. Aside from odd bits of vandalism, the only other destruction in the whole length between Sandown and Newport was a subsidence where the line bordered the river between Horringford and Merstone.

So enjoyable did we find our excursion over the erstwhile Isle of Wight (Newport Junction) Railway, that we made another expedition from Ventnor West to Newport a couple of months later. We gained permission for this also from the Newport offices, but were told that certain portions of the trackbed between Ventnor West and Merstone were not now in railway hands. Nothing daunted, and prepared for many a removed bridge span, we set out. The station building at Ventnor West was as yet derelict, with one of the windows continuing to announce "Buffet". It crossed my mind

that this could scarcely have been the busiest catering enterprise in the world, even at the height of the station's usage!

Four years had elapsed since the track was lifted, and mother nature had taken over with a vengeance. The platforms at Ventnor West were all but invisible, and the stretch along the Undercliff almost impassable. We persevered, however, and the route became a little less overgrown as we climbed towards the tunnel at St Lawrence. Ten yards inside the tunnel a persistent buzzing pointed to a bee or wasp's nest, and we passed under the sound as rapidly as possible, eyes straining in the dark for the first glimmer of light which would tell us we were rounding the bend.

The rest of the walk to Merstone, although interesting in a scenic way, was not desperately rewarding from a railway point-of-view, although it was interesting to discover that Whitwell had once possessed two platforms. I think it was about here that we proceeded unwittingly into some of the territory "no longer in railway hands". There was some kind problem with a number of officious goats and their owner, and the "We have permission from Mr Gardener" routine failed dismally, as well it should have done. The response from the goat-man was along the lines of "Who the hell is he?", and we trespassed rapidly away, watched by suspicious eyes.

Rural idyll aside, it soon became obvious that one stretch of disused trackbed is generally much like another, and we were pleased to meet the rails again at Merstone.

Later in the year, a couple of the party (of whom I was one) investigated the remains of the Freshwater line, aided by the use of a borrowed car. The track had been lifted only relatively recently, but except for a reminder of the relative solitude of West Wight, I noted little of new interest. We observed that the booking office at Freshwater station still sold rail tickets, that W H Smith's bookstall there continued to be open for business and that the goods yard was still used by the coal merchant, who now had his supplies delivered by road, but the impression was very much one of a territory that had very much learned to live without its railway, and, in truth, was not missing it much.

In spite of the fact that the only lingering evidence of the existence of an increasing amount of the Island's railway network was the vacant earthworks and some structures, this still didn't deter quite a number of us from imagining, and almost believing from the short press reports which appeared occasionally about local takeovers and such like, that there was going to be some kind of Island transport revolution, and that most things would eventually be reinstated in some shape or form.

I don't know at what age nostalgia sets in, but there is no doubt that we hoped against hope for a reversion to the days when the Island's prosperity seemed to hinge on the activities of the railways, and when sympathetic local managements attempted, at least from time to time, to tune performance to local need.

There was little attractive to us about our system being governed by an administration consisting of people who would nowadays be called "grey men", sitting in the British Railways HQ in London, heedless of our uniqueness and the part which our railways continued to play in so many daily lives. In saying this, I am perfectly sure that I am replaying the tapes of so many of the railwaymen with whom we spoke, but no matter. We wanted some kind of creative solution to the railway question, and if that meant local takeover, so much the better. The time for this, however, was not right, and like so many local communities in the fifties and sixties, we stood by and watched as, little by little, the grey men took out our pride and joy piece by piece, by stupid bureaucratic rules, expenditure which seemed irrelevant, or simply by beating a cowardly retreat in the face of the changing transport habits of the population.

The south portal of the disused St. Lawrence tunnel. 12 July 1958.

Top - *Yarmouth, viewed towards Newport, the former Down platform on the right.*
Bottom - *Ningwood, seen from a Freshwater train.*

Both by Denis Callender in the early 1950s.

Left - A Sandown train having just crossed the viaduct at Newport and about to pass through the lattice girders of Coppins Bridge, circa 1950.

This page, top - The original brick viaduct for the Sandown line, around 1950. The great scar of Shide Quarry, for years the provider of an enormous amount of chalk traffic to the railway, is in the background.

This page, bottom - 1952 carriage notice.   *All by Denis Callender*

The Ryde-Newport-Cowes quadrant of the Island was the least familiar for me. Newport was visited usually by 'bus, and then not very often. Cowes remained a mystery for far too long, except for the odd visit, again, because of apparent convenience, by 'bus, and it is surprising to look back and realise that it was not until early in 1958 that I ventured thus far by train. There was an irrational foregone conclusion that the best way from south Wight to north Wight after the demise of the Sandown-Newport line was bound to be by road, because it looked reasonably straightforward on the map. Once investigated, however, this was not so, and even allowing for the change of trains at Ryde St. Johns, the journey times between Shanklin and Newport were not significantly different. Neither was the fare, and I suspect the reasonably sensible pricing of cheap day returns kept a certain amount of through traffic between both lines alive. Aside from the issue of transport methodology, though, one of the major reasons for my late entry into Cowes by train was simply because it was outside normal territory, and business or pleasure seldom required the trip (added to which there was always the issue of Island distances....).

The journey was eventually made, past the deserted station at Ashey where the route of the long-abandoned siding to the quarry and the racecourse was clearly delineated by trees and fences, past the curious ground level buildings and bare island platform of Haven Street, past the remains of Wootton and Whippingham stations to arrive at a Newport that was still tolerably busy. Passengers and parcels on the platform, coal being unloaded in the yard, but a broad expanse of largely empty tracks on what might be termed the "railway" side of the site. Then on to Cement Mills, with the points still down and a siding disappearing into undergrowth, and the discovery that the Halt still existed - one up again on Michael Robbins for his use of the past tense in this respect! - past Medina Wharf - tiny staff platform, apparent acres of sidings full of wagons dipping down to the wharf and gantries - the short hitherto undiscovered Gas House Siding, Mill Hill, the tunnel and out into the sunshine of Cowes. And there, gently hissing in the sidings, was No. 3, having disposed of a coal wagon or two.

Encountering her bunker-first I suddenly realised how old-fashioned she looked, with wooden toolbox and cab narrower than the tanks. Swathed in steam, she departed with

the brake-van shortly after our arrival, for another stint of shunting and resting amongst the coal wagons at Medina.

Cowes station still boasted a Southern Railway notice outside, and although close to the centre of the town seemed quietly in repose. There were few passengers, and after the O2 which brought us went through the routine of pushing the coaches clear of the release cross-over, moving forward again to clear the points and run round the train whilst the guard used his brake to allow the coaches to roll back towards the buffers down the gradient under their own momentum ready for the return to Ryde, silence descended, save for the chirping of sparrows in the awning and the sound of the shovelling of coal from the sidings.

Up till then, Medina Wharf and Cement Mills had been merely interesting sounding place names in a book, with their presence indicated by the "Mineral Line" symbol on the 1939 one-inch Ordnance Map we had at home. The latter gave no real indication of the size or complexity of either location, although there was a second line tantalisingly shown crossing back under the railway at Cement Mills, presumably to a chalk quarry.

I was never able to pay the Cement Mills the attention they seemed to deserve, but I did get to know Medina Wharf quite well. Whilst the coal imported into the Island was transported at least in part by rail, Medina would be full, and save for trip working to Newport and Cowes during the day, there would always be a locomotive present. This was the work for which the E1's were used, but when they disappeared, the O2's seemed to cope well enough.

Although still busy, the Wharf was a little like the exterior of Ryde works. Things obviously <u>did</u> happen, but one seldom saw much action taking place. The sidings were generally crowded, and every revenue-earning wagon was an open one, full or empty. It was here that I caught up with the two remaining IWR 10-ton open wagons, allocated by now to the Motive Power Department for transport of loco coal. A real glimpse of the past, these, with axle-boxes cast with their original owner's initials, wooden under-frames and wheels with split spokes.

A highlight of the late summer of 1958 was a visit to Newport and all its acres, again with permission of the authorities. The station foreman was detailed to escort a friend and

Opposite - Newport North signal box in 1952. The lines to Smallbrook Junction and for Sandown use the platforms on the left. The Freshwater branch diverged off to the right.

Denis Callender, early 1950s.

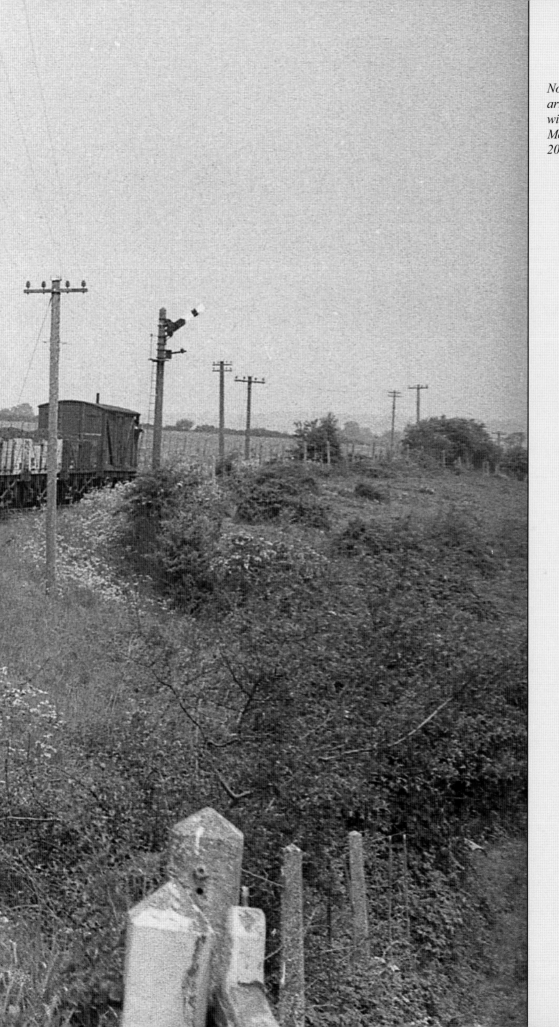

No. 32 'Bonchurch'
arriving at Newport
with a freight from
Medina Wharf.
20 May 1961.

Newport from the north. The locomotive depot is visible on the left.   *Denis Callender, early 1950s.*

myself. He was a long-serving railway employee, steeped in pessimism for the future. "All this," he said, embracing the whole Newport complex with gestures, "All this will be gone in five years. You wait and see." He was very nearly right, but even with the obviously run-down state of much that we saw, we couldn't really credit such a view. Diminished, perhaps, but not extinct, was our view - a wrong one, as it turned out.

Although emptier than in former times, there was still much of interest at Newport. It came as a pleasant surprise to find part of the old IWC works still in use as a paint shop for coaches. We viewed the automatic pump used to raise water for locomotives to the storage tank, discovered the aforementioned six-wheel crane lurking in the depths of the disused locomotive shed, found grounded coach bodies of considerable antiquity, and were introduced to the corrugated-iron shack near the road entrance to the Hunny Hill yard that once housed, apparently, the Freshwater, Yarmouth and Newport Railway's offices. Our guide was able to break through his pessimism enough to tell us a few stories from the old days, and with the encouragement of imagination, and in spite of the quiet and the feeling that things were being run down, it was still not that hard to picture the whole place as it was when the shed was open for twenty-four hours a day, and there was always some kind of activity going on.

Around midday No. 4 arrived with the freight from Medina - three 10-ton wagons of coal and a brake van. She proceeded to deposit these in the merchant's sidings adjoining the station approach, not by discreet run-round and loose-shunting, but by fly-shunting, which I had never witnessed before and which was something to behold. Having left the brake van out of harm's way, the locomotive accelerated sharply for a few yards towards the yard and then shut-off steam to slacken the couplings, enabling the guard, producing some nifty work with the shunter's pole, to uncouple the rear wagon. The locomotive with the remaining wagons then accelerated into neutral territory, and a member of the station staff quickly changed the points behind them to guide the uncoupled wagon towards its appropriate home with the guard in hot pursuit to pin down the brakes when the stopping place was reached. This process worked well twice, but the third wagon, whether over-enthusiastically accelerated or not I can't remember, got away, and with the guard struggling unsuccessfully to un-ship the brake lever, arrived at its destination with a bang which echoed around the whole station, and a cloud of coal dust. Such was the noise that damage must have been done, but no, everything was apparently unharmed, except for the guard's pride, which received further damage from the taunts of the engine crew who had observed the pantomime with glee. So had two onlookers on the platform, who continued to watch whilst No 4 visited the water tower, gathered up the brake van and pottered off again in the direction of Medina.

Later in the year visits were paid to some of the former providers of freight to the Island railways. The chalk quarry in Ashey Down, whose traffic was the cause of much consternation when a proposal was made to upgrade the tramway from Ryde St John's to an extended pier for freight import

Newport locomotive depot. In the view above, No. 30 'Shorwell' is outside the shed. In the bottom view, Nos. 35 'Freshwater' and 36 'Carisbrooke' are resplendent in newly applied BR black livery, but as yet without the BR totem or nameplates. This suggests that the photographs were taken shortly after their arrival in the Island in April 1949."   Denis Callender

and export in 1874, had its entrance tunnel still extant, but not much else visible because of filling and collapsing sides. Entrance tunnels seemed to be the norm for the rail-connected quarries, and the much bigger hole in the downs at Shide which used to supply the Cement Mills also had one, still at this time accessible and dripping. The Shide quarry still had sleepers denoting where the tracks had been, but not much else was left of a formerly prosperous industry. Well derelict and overgrown, too, was Gunville Brickworks, although the site of the siding could be traced amongst the brambles.

As remarked earlier, by the mid-fifties the freight traffic on the Island had dwindled to little but coal. Items like tar, cattle, timber and sugar beet were relatively recent casualties, but the lorry had not completed its advance of convenience merely with these. The ease with which the areas formerly served by closed lines had transferred their entire goods allegiance to the road, albeit compulsorily, showed that local rail-borne freight in moderate quantities was by no means the only option in the mid-twentieth century. Nevertheless, slightly melancholy visits to the sites of former activity gave a good impression of how things might have been in their heyday when the Island railways were largely unchallenged in their territory as common carriers.

Opposite, top left - No. 16 'Ventnor' arriving at Newport with a train from Cowes. 21 April 1958.

Opposite, top right - No 4 'Wroxall' takes a break from shunting after the incident of the wagon that got away. 1 September 1958.

Opposite bottom - Newly outshopped No. 32 'Bonchurch' pauses during shunting operations at Newport. 20 May 1961

This page - No. 28 'Ashey' taking water prior to departing for Ryde. 16 April 1960.

Above - No. 14 'Fishbourne' arriving at Newport with a train for Cowes, 18 May 1964.

Right - No. 4 'Wroxall' taking water in the former Freshwater bay at Newport September 1958, prior to returning to work at Medina Wharf.

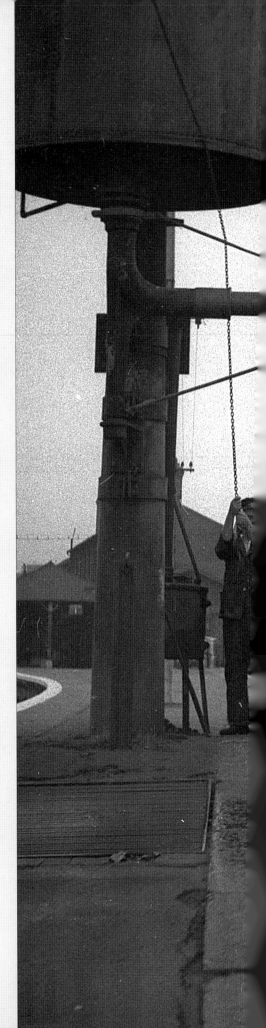

Opposite top - *August 1949 and No. 25 'Godshill' arrives at Newport with a train from Cowes. At this stage the engine was in Southern green but portraying 'British Railways' ownership details.*   *Denis Callender*
Opposite bottom - *Two ex-IWCR water tanks, Nos. 443S and 428S converted for weed killing are seen in the sidings at Newport, 29 August 1959.*

This page, top right - *A former LBSCR 10 ton open wagon, No. S19005 at Newport. 29 August 1959.*
Bottom left - *Ex-LCDR passenger guard and luggage van, withdrawn from passenger service as No. 1008 in 1950, and re-designated as service vehicle DS3185 derelict at Medina Wharf, 1 September 1958. It had arrived on the Island in 1930.*
Bottom right - *A former LBSCR cattle wagon, converted into a 10 ton van in 1935 and numbered, S46926, at Newport, 29 August 1959.*

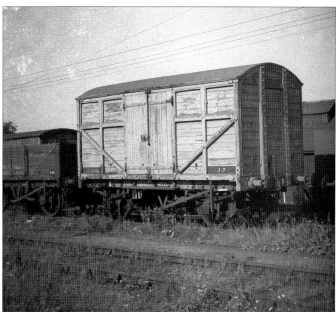

Top - *Goods working at Cowes. No. 3 'Ryde' leaving the station to return to Medina Wharf after bringing in coal. 21 April 1958.*

Bottom - *Brake van No. S56047 at Newport, 20 May 1961.*

Right - *Having arrived at Cowes from Ryde, No. 25 'Godshill' is ready to push the carriage stock back clear of the engine release crossover, 16 April 1960.*

*Cowes, circa 1950. No. 25
'Godshill' has pushed the coaching stock clear of the crossover and will now run forward onto the single line towards Mill Hill. The coaches will then be allowed to drop back towards the buffers under gravity. The disc signal applied to both the platform and crossover lines.*

Notice that in the view on the previous page, this same engine is facing the opposite way. With no turntables on the Island this could only be achieved as a result of having used what was in effect a triangle travelling via the Merstone route.

Denis Callender

Above - *No. 25 'Godshill' again, but this time at Shanklin. The signal-man is receiving the tablet pouch from what was a terminating service from Ryde. 28 June 1958.*

Left - *'Jarge', the Shanklin outside porter, with his barrow ready for hire. 23 May 1959.*

There was a feeling about my final year as a resident of the Island that I find difficult to describe. I have said before that there was the certain knowledge that things would have to change in my life, and that change somehow seemed to reflect the change that was going to have to happen sooner or later to the railways.

As far as my own life was concerned, I should have had the feeling of expansion, of exploring pastures new. There was certainly a youthful looking forward to new experiences, but at the same time there was a kind of desperate realisation that I was about to lose something that would never be recovered. Surely this was about an environment to which, in spite of any shortcomings, I had become attached, about relationships that were carefree in a late teenage way, but at the same time of enormous and sometimes harrowing importance? Surely it was also about losing the safe fun of being in a co-ed environment (academic idler I certainly was, but it had its social compensations!). Mainly, however, the feeling almost of panic that contemplation of the impending change brought with it was about parting with too much at once - a treasured portion of youth was to go at the same time as I was to relinquish tried and trusted ways of life. The railway was one of these, and I found the whole business unbearably hard. Even now, if I could put the clock back, I think I should turn the hands to early in 1959....

I hung on to every memory. Like the cold dark winter recesses of the Ryde end of the up platform at Shanklin where over some weeks I bade the girlfriend from Ryde "Goodnight" prior to seeing her on to the last train home, watching out of the corner of my eye the similar antics of another young blood ensconced in the parcels entrance on the other platform as he did the same with his girl from Ventnor. The train pulling in, and our emergence from the dark not quite quickly enough to avoid the knowing smiles of the driver and fireman.

Actually, we didn't do badly on the Ryde-Ventnor line for later evening trains. The last working out of Ventnor left there at 9.40pm, thus meaning that I could enjoy the girlfriend's company until 9.52. The young blood on the down platform was a little luckier, his girl's train being the 9.43pm from Ryde Pier Head, not departing from Shanklin until 10.08. This was also the last connecting working of the day with a train from Waterloo – the 6.50pm fast service to Portsmouth Harbour, which gave a good long day for sightseeing, shopping or business in the metropolis. The final train returned from Ventnor as an empty stock work-ing, and I can recall its rapid dark and rapid progress over Lake bridge when I happened to be in the vicinity one night, its ghostly blackness broken only by a spectral glow from the locomotive cab and a glimmer of dim electricity from the guard's part of the train.

There was the religious plotting of the diagrams for every train movement of each day. This information was provided partly by our own observations, partly by those of the mother of a friend (who was under the strictest orders to watch every train from the window of the kitchen of their house which backed on to the railway at Sandown, and to note the locomotive numbers and times) and partly by another enthusiast from Ryde who gave us the daily low-down on the shed and works situation there. He was also a useful source of rumour, having an uncle who worked as a fitter in the works.

Rumours were more rife than they had ever been, or perhaps I was just more attuned to them. They started in the autumn of 1958 with the news that four locomotives were to be stored at Sandown for the winter. The previous year Newport shed had been used, but now outdoor storage was to be adopted. Ashey had been suggested as a possible venue, but rumour relayed that Sandown was the favourite, and, sure enough, Nos 18, 32, and 16 duly arrived on the daily freight on the 9th, 10th and 21st of October respectively, followed by No 27 on November 14th.

At the end of 1958 there were strong rumours that Nos 3 and 4 and one O2 were to be scrapped. Though premature, these were not too inaccurate, and as already mentioned No 3 was broken up during the late summer of 1959. No 4, although withdrawn a year later, lingered virtually whole into 1961, but there was no withdrawal of any further O2 until 1962, eighteen months ahead of the start of the holocaust which left only No 24 intact after 1967. The E1's may have had a habit of exceeding their due time; pieces of No 1 in the shape of smokebox door and buffers still lingered at the end of the coal-stage road at Ryde St. Johns until the end of 1958, although she was withdrawn in mid-1957.

It was clear by this time to anyone who knew anything about locomotives at all that with the best will in the world the skilled men at Ryde could not go on patching up the O2's and the E1's, whilst the latter still existed, *ad infinitum*, and that if the railway was to survive in any form, something would have to be done about the motive power situation.

I remember the last time I saw No 3 on the morning freight to Ventnor setting off from Sandown up the gradient to Lake

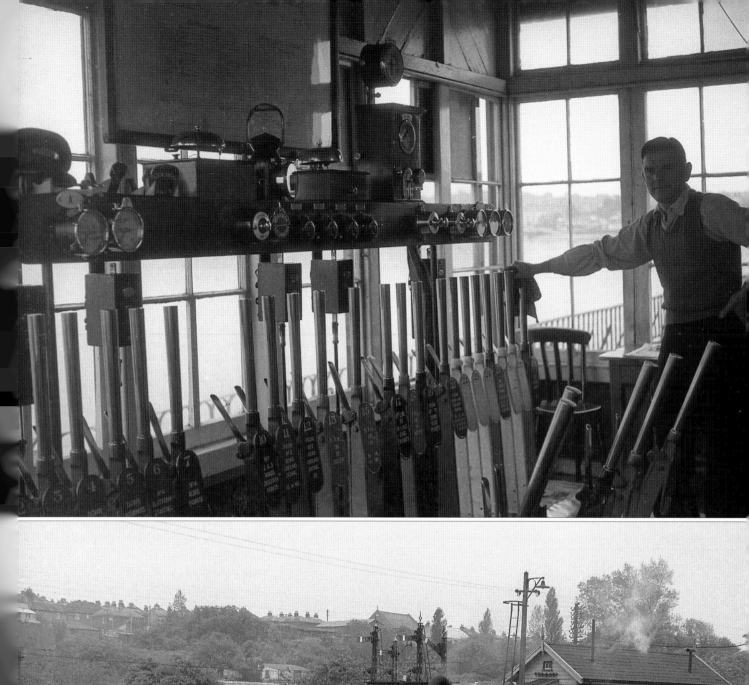

Bridge with steam leaking from almost every part of her anatomy.

Breakdowns occurred, although not as frequently as they might have done, and I believe that this was due to the dedication of those at Ryde works. The only one which touched me personally was on March 18th 1959, when arrival at Shanklin station for the journey to school was greeted by the news that there were no trains running. No 29 heading the 7.40am from Ryde Pier Head to Ventnor had stalled towards the top of Apse Bank with a fractured piston head, and thus there was no return working from Ventnor at 8.40am. The 8.35am from Ryde Pier Head in the charge of No 17 was held at St. Johns for a few minutes, while No 28 was removed from the yard and quickly attached to the front of the train, which then proceeded as usual to Shanklin. Here No 17 ran round the train, and returned with it to Ryde, whilst No 28 went on towards Ventnor, and propelled the train with the injured No 29 on to Wroxall, where the latter was parked on the siding and her fire dropped. I presume that No 28 ran round the train at Wroxall, and then took it on to Ventnor.

We made our way to school by 'bus that day, and then, taking advantage of the flexibility of being in the sixth form, a friend and myself took an extended lunch hour to visit Wroxall in his parents' car to see No 29 for ourselves. We found her cooling and forlorn, with the offending piston head removed and laid on the footplate by her smokebox. Supporting the theory that every cloud has a silver lining, a member of the Wroxall station staff was improving the shining hour by diligently filling the station coal buckets from the locomotive's bunker. No 29 was removed to Ryde for repair during the afternoon, presumably with a much reduced coal supply!

Another rumour of early 1959 suggested that ex-LNER J72 0-6-0T's built after the war to a NER design were a possibility as replacements for the ailing and almost life-expired O2's, but nothing more was heard of the idea. A further rumour, quickly confirmed this time, concerned the scrapping of seventeen coaches in the spring of 1959, with balancing rumours of the possibility of BR standard non-corridor stock coming to the rescue. In the spring of 1959 there was also strong talk of the Newport and Cowes line being closed, and being told of the movement of the Engineer's Department to Ryde seemed to add credence to this.

It was not all bad news. Some positive things were happening. In January 1959 an Engineer's Department train turned up at Sandown, and whilst the locomotive - No 31 - took water at the Newport line water crane (was she the last engine to do so?), new sleepers were unloaded on to Platform Three. The train then headed off to Shanklin, depositing sleepers at several points along the way. The following day No 20 turned up with rails and more sleepers, which were off-loaded into the six-foot way between platforms one and

two. Locomotives undergoing major overhaul were still being turned out beautifully, and cab interiors were finished in buff above the waist line and the frames of some were painted vermilion on the inside. The ex-LBSC 10-ton crane had a repaint, too, although its match-truck went untouched.

As spring blossomed and turned into the most glorious of summers, the camera was disinterred again, and every Saturday, and some Sundays, saw expeditions to every railway installation and location you could name. Saturdays were still incredibly busy, and it was hard to believe when seeing the procession of crowded trains on the Ventnor line that the railways were anything but thriving. Together with the Ryde stations and Brading, Sandown and Shanklin saw continual comings and goings, and in addition to the through workings, the termination of one train an hour at the latter two places meant that traffic was interestingly increased with the palaver of the locomotive running around its train and then depositing it in the right platform for departure, without getting in the way of the two trains every hour destined for Ventnor.

It wasn't only the interiors of the principal stations on the Ventnor line that were busy. Because they were at the backs of the towns they served, passengers often had to cover quite long distances to their hotels and guest houses. The more well-heeled gave the taxis considerable trade, and there was always a string of people on foot to and from their destinations in sometimes quite distant parts of the resorts.

An interesting piece of local enterprise was visible on summer Saturdays at Sandown and Shanklin. Each station forecourt was occupied by boys of varying ages with an interesting selection of home-made trolleys, in which second-hand timber and pram wheels featured strongly, who, in return for a small consideration, would cart passengers' luggage and guide them to their holiday accommodation.

I don't suppose that this youthful entrepreneurism was limited to the Island resorts, but at Shanklin there was someone truly unique. At Shanklin we had "Jarge". Now Jarge was getting on in years, and he was a genuine "Outside Porter", with, moreover, a polished brass plate on his battered hat to prove it. He also had a proper two-wheeled barrow, well painted in red and green. I recall that he wore boots and leather gaiters, but had a generally rather down-at-heel appearance. I think that he was available for hire all the year round, but on summer Saturdays he was more prominent and had much competition from the boys in the timber and pram wheels department. The competition was not purely economic, either, and in the brief quiet times he would sometimes be ribbed unmercifully by the little terrors, who, sensing that Jarge seemed to be a little closer to their own intellectual level than to an adult one, knew just how to wind him up. The brass hat badge and the barrow led me to believe that Jarge was a throwback to a former era, and may well have been the last of other similar operators who per-

Opposite top - Signalman Vic Hailes on duty at Ryde Pier Head, 19 May 1961.
Opposite bottom - Nos. 20 'Shanklin' and 33 'Bembridge' at Ryde shed, 19 May 1961.

Winter storage at Brickfield Sidings, Sandown.
Above - 26 March 1959, Nos: 27 'Merstone', 16 'Ventnor', 32 'Bonchurch' and 18 'Ningwood'.
Right - *17 April 1960, Nos 22 'Brading', 20 'Shanklin', 30 'Shorwell' and 29 'Alverstone'.*

formed at the station in the days of the Isle of Wight Railway.

Holidaymakers were not the only ones who used the trains, and there was still a large body of locals who travelled all the year round because it was the most convenient way to do so. The Island system had its own rush-hours and busy times for regular passengers, just as the mainland railways did.

That summer I had splendid sessions at all the stations on the Ventnor line, whiling away sunlit hours photographing the scene and talking with railwaymen. The Cowes line did not escape attention, either, and visits were paid to see the goings-on in that part of the Island, and to seek out interesting rolling-stock and new bits of history.

School closed, the days in the sun wore on, the photographs accumulated. As the evenings shortened, so did my time as an Island resident, and in early September I sadly departed for pastures new, and the pleasures of working life in

Slough, where I began to unearth treasures of a different kind, usually involving copper chimney caps and brass safety valve casings. Rich though these were, however, they were not a patch on the things I had left, and I managed to revisit the Island in both 1960 and 1961. On both occasions I was pleased enough to see that many things remained unaltered, although the smell of decay was thicker in the air with each passing year.

In 1960 the Sandown-Newport line was lifted, and Coppins Bridge dismantled. I noted utter devastation at St. Helens and Bembridge. The sidings at Sandown were again host to winter-stored O2's, this time Nos 22, 20, 30 and 29, but alongside them was a row of wagons marked "Condemned". In a brighter vein, the new breakdown van was at last finished. I stayed with a friend who had pursued his interest in railways into the real world, and had joined BR on the engineering side. He suggested to me that there were plans afoot for the modification of BR Standard Class 2 2-6-2T's for Island work, and this was an exciting prospect. In fact, his-

Ventnor from the approach road, 17 May 1964,
still with its 'Southern Railway' sign.

tory reveals that it almost came to pass.

By 1961 all coaching stock had reassumed Southern Green, and looked the better for it. Aside from this things were much as before, but the Class 2's had not materialised, and there was no-one who didn't expect to see the writing on the wall at any time.

I paid a further visit, this time from the West Country, in 1964, just ahead of the writing's appearance, and that was my last acquaintance with things as they were. Then there were announcements, and public enquiries, accusations, claims and counter-claims. BR gave in a little, but the Cowes line and the route from Shanklin to Ventnor were no more. The latter, particularly, seemed like a vindictive act of vandalism, still regretted by many over forty years later. Gone were many of my stamping-grounds of happy memory, gone was the echoing well of Ventnor, and gone the dank sooty smell of the tunnel. And then gone were my sturdy O2's, no longer to shout their way up Apse and to greet the world at Ryde Pier Head with their hooters.

I ought, I suppose, have attended the last rites, but somehow the inevitability of them made them seem slightly superfluous. I think in truth that my last rites were in 1959, and all that came after was like the failing breaths that come between the valediction and the final peace. I could have been there, but it would probably have been too much to stand.

Superannuated tube trains came. Track layouts were simplified. People still travelled, as I did on honeymoon in 1971 (remember the Merstone signal register?!). Slight awakening. Rail blue gave way to the crisp toothpaste-like livery of Network SouthEast, and a new "Lake" was opened. In time a second generation of superannuated tube cars appeared, still used every day by goodly numbers of local travellers, including for a time my sister, who had returned to live in the Island for two or three years. And those splendid people at Haven Street, having rescued a little of the essence of the Isle of Wight railways in their golden days, flourished, and pushed the line from their unlikely headquarters back to Smallbrook. They even persuaded Network SouthEast to open a station there.

Eventually different liveries appeared on the trains from Ryde to Shanklin, now franchised to Island Line, which regularly takes a high place in national punctuality tables. It's nice to know that the rump of the once splendid system with which I was so familiar is still famous for something.

Above - *Ex-LSWR passenger van No. 1279S (original running number 1000), in use as a breakdown van at Ryde St Johns. 27 August 1958.*
Opposite page - *No. 18 'Ningwood' emerging from Ventnor Tunnel whilst in the process of running round its train. 20 June 1959.*

EPILOGUE

Who knows, but that things may yet change more, and the fabric of time become repaired? If it is easy to hope, might it also be possible? From time to time I visit the Island still, nowadays for work, and I seldom let a visit pass without making a detour to Haven Street. I stand amongst the activity that has turned this rural no-man's-land into a thriving railway centre, and cheer the efforts of those responsible. I look up the line towards where things have not changed so very much, and hear a hooter and revisit those times so fresh in the mind that in a flash I am back to my teens.

I have a curious feeling that in some ways we ain't seen nothing yet. When we do, I hope that I shall be around......

10

2

BRITISH RAILWAYS

WARNING
PASSENGERS
ARE STRICTLY
FORBIDDEN
TO ENTER THE
STATION
THIS WAY

Left - No. 21 'Sandown' hurries thought the station of the same name with a non-stop train for Shanklin. 14 June 1958. The crossing in the foreground is the one that was used by children passing between the split sites of Sandown Grammar School.

Above - The driver of No. 24 'Calbourne' oiling its Westinghouse pump at Ventnor. 17 May 1964.

Above - A perfect summer's day. No. 18 'Ningwood' west of Wootton with a train for Cowes. 17 May 1964.

Bottom - No. 33 'Bembridge' passing Smallbrook Junction, the point of divergence of the Ventnor and Newport lines, with a train from Ventnor, 20 May 1961. The signal arms have been restored for the summer service but are not yet in use.

Page 89 - *No. 32 'Bonchurch' awaiting departure from Ryde with a summer working to Cowes.*
Opposite, top - *No. 16 'Ventnor' between Ryde Pier Head and Ryde Esplanade with a train for Cowes.*
Opposite, bottom - *With the Gas Works in the background No. 26 'Whitwell' enters Ryde St Johns Road.*
Top - *A summer's day at Ryde Esplanade and No. 27 'Merstone' with an all-stations to Ventnor.*
Bottom - *Smallbrook Junction: the signalman giving out the tablet for the section to Brading.*

All Bob Winkworth collection, probably from around 1960.

Pages 92/93 - *No. 31 ' Chale', but without at least one nameplate, and No. 22 'Brading' cross at Wroxall. Probably 1965 or 1966.*

Tony Molyneaux

Above - *Reflections on earlier days: Merstone receiving the attention of the scrap merchants, probably early summer 1960.*

John Bailey

Opposite top - *No. 17 'Seaview' and No. 18 'Ningwood' meet at Ryde St. Johns, early 1960's.*   *KR collection*

Opposite centre - *No. 27 'Merstone' leaving Sandown for Ryde in the early 1960's.*   *Bob Winkworth collection*

Opposite bottom - *Cowes, with No. 18 'Ningwood awaiting departure for Newport and Ryde, early 1960's.*   *KR collection*

Changing times at Ryde St. Johns, late 1966 / early 1967.

Bob Winkworth collection